"LeRoy 'Boots' Battle has been a champion all of his life, demonstrating integrity, selfless service, and excellence in all he attempted. These values continue to influence many who respect and admire his life's mission of mentoring, flight, education, music, and community service. He creates an environment of peace and harmony in all he represents. He is a diplomat extraordinaire!"

Cora M. "Tess" Spooner—Past National President, Tuskegee Airmen, Inc.

"LeRoy Battle's life story is at times poignant, funny, sad, and adventurous. He has truly lived an amazing life and this book is something to be treasured by one and all."

J. A. Hitchcock—Author and Cyber Crime Expert;
President, Working to Halt Online Abuse (WHOA) and WHOA-KTD (Kids/Teen Division)

"Mr. LeRoy Battle—a Tuskegee Airman, a jazz musician, and an educator—is a living American legend of the personal courage, the collective activism, and the community mobilization that many of our elders engaged in to succeed. Individuals who did more with less than we have today, and who still encourage us to continue our BEAT!!!"

Dr. Mary Brown-Scott—Director, The Book Bridge Project and
The African American Studies Institute, Prince George's Community College

"LeRoy Battle embodies the essence of an American generation that stood for greatness. His talents encompass the role of historian, professional musician, teacher, and civil rights activist. It is my sincere honor to call a gentleman of this magnitude friend, and it is my privilege to publish this memoir of his remembrances."

Sarah Sherman McGrail—Publisher, Cozy Harbor Press

And the Beat Goes On...

Remembrances of a Cosmopolite

by LeRoy A. Battle

*Educator, Jazz Musician,
Tuskegee Airman, Composer, Author*

Cover photograph and book photographs
courtesy of Leo P. Heppner

**COZY
HARBOR
PRESS**

Printed by J.S. McCarthy Printers; Augusta, Maine
Design and production by Tim Seymour Designs, LLC; Camden, Maine
Cover art by James A. Taliana; Boothbay Harbor, Maine

"BEST WISHES"

LeRoy A. Battle

4/12/14

Dedication

....

I dedicate this book to my long-time friend
Wilbur C. Tolson and his charming wife Ernestine,
who had read my first book, *Easier Said*, more than
once, and knew that some pertinent experiences had
been omitted. They suggested that, if I wrote another
book, those experiences should definitely be included.
Another book had never crossed my mind; however,
Wilbur would not let me rest. He arranged for me to
appear on the radio station WMAL in Washington, DC,
where he worked, and he also set up a book signing for
me at the Forestville Mall. Wilbur's vision of the
continued need for another book was the fuel
that energized me into action.

Preface

As I begin my second book, *And the Beat Goes On*, I feel that a greater in-depth examination of my ancestry is needed. In retrospect, I know that the genes of many people affect the person that I am today. This closer look at my ancestors, therefore, will help me to better understand why I consequently think and act as I do and, subsequently, some of the factors influencing the present "me."

Also, comments from different people jogged my memory of things not included in my first book, *Easier Said*, about other happenings and/or prior experiences. Because of these omissions, I feel compelled to fill in those "potholes" along my highway of knowledge.

Such events recorded herein are selected to be as descriptive and realistic as possible, bringing together all of the salient happenings in my life and the subsequent changes in my immediate and distant goals, thus *And the Beat Goes On*.

About the Author

LeRoy Andrew Battle, a native of New York, New York, became involved with music at approximately 10 years of age. His formal training in music began in the Boy Scouts when he became a member of the Drum and Bugle Corps. It was there that he began to learn to read music. He attended P.S. 35 Elementary School in Harlem, New York, and the Stephen Decatur Junior High School in Brooklyn, New York. He then enrolled in Alexander Hamilton High School for Boys in Brooklyn, New York. It was at Hamilton that music "bubbled" up to become the main emphasis of his thinking and doing; music has remained so.

In 1938, at the age of 17, LeRoy won the coveted Philharmonic Scholarship for the Borough of Brooklyn, by playing at Carnegie Hall in the contest. This enabled him to study with the concert master and premier tympanist of the New York Philharmonic Orchestra, Saul Goodman. LeRoy's classes with Mr. Goodman were held at the Metropolitan Opera House. Following his graduation from Alexander Hamilton High School, he matriculated at the Radio and Maritime Trade Center in the day and took advanced courses in music theory and music education at night at City College of New York.

On August 23, 1943, LeRoy was inducted into the service at Camp Upton, Long Island, New York. After Camp Upton, he was stationed at the following Army airfields: Keesler Field, Mississippi, for Basic Training; Tuskegee Institute in Alabama for Air Cadet Training; Tyndall Field in Florida for Gunnery Training; Midland Field in Texas for Bombardier/Navigation Training; Godman Field in Kentucky for Advanced Bombardier/Navigation Training; Walterboro Field in South Carolina for Over Water, Air to Air, Gunnery and Bombardier/Navigation Training; and Freeman Field, Seymour, Indiana. At Freeman Field, he took part in the "Mutiny at Freeman Field." He was one of the first 19 Negro officers arrested for going into a White officers club on April 5, 1945. He was threatened with court martial and hanging for disobeying a direct order in the time of war not to enter the officers club. Still under arrest, he was returned to Godman Field in Kentucky. Meanwhile, his 616th Squadron was deleted from the 477th Bomb Group. At the same time, all of the officers under arrest were released. Lieutenant Battle went next to Tuskegee Army Air Field for Pilot Training and then to Maxwell Army Field Base for discharge from the service on October 13, 1945.

Following his honorable discharge from the service, LeRoy enrolled at the Juilliard School of Music. He attended Juilliard in the day and participated in Columbia University's Marching Band Program in the evenings and on the weekends. In the fall of 1946, he enrolled at Morgan State College in Baltimore, Maryland, graduating in June 1950 with a major in instrumental music and a minor in education.

LeRoy's first job placement following his graduation was at Douglass Elementary Junior Senior Colored High School in Upper Marlboro, Maryland, where he was the instrumental music teacher from 1950 to 1968. Mr. Robert F. Frisby was the principal there. During this time, he organized the Douglass Eagles Marching Bands, A & B, the Concert Band, the Stage Band, and the Band Boosters Club. Mr. Battle's first official act as a teacher was to write to all of the publishing companies that served the school, informing them that there was only one Douglass Elementary Junior Senior High School in Upper Marlboro, and that they should drop the term "Colored" when sending communications to the school. The companies were herein notified that if they failed to comply with the request, Douglass would terminate its business association with them. The companies readily acquiesced and sent their field representatives to apologize.

While at Douglass, Battle pursued his graduate studies at the University of Maryland, College Park, receiving his Master of Education degree in June 1961. He did further postgraduate studies at Bowie State College from 1968 to 1970 with majors in education and psychology.

In 1968, Battle became a guidance counselor at Benjamin Foulois Junior High School, Morningside, Maryland, with Mr. Harold Bayes as his principal. He then became vice principal at Suitland Junior High School in 1970, with Dr. Milton Bailey as his principal. The Board of Education attempted to move Mr. Battle to another school that was experiencing student unrest, as he dealt with problem students and parents excellently. However, the faculty at Suitland Junior High wrote up a petition and went to the Board of Education, urging them to let Mr. Battle remain at Suitland.

Next, Mr. Battle became vice principal at James Madison Junior High School, Upper Marlboro, in 1972, with Mr. Glenn S. Lesher as his principal. Battle felt that he could be of a greater and broader benefit to the students as a counselor rather than as vice principal, so he left school administration and returned to counseling. From 1974 to 1978, he was counselor at Surrattsville Junior High, Clinton, Maryland, with Mr. Charles McIntosh as his principal. In 1978, he retired from the teaching profession.

His other professional involvements have been many and varied. From 1966 to 1982, he was a member of the Washington Redskins Marching Band. In 1982, he became the official manager of the Altones Swing Combo. From the age of 29 on, he had been a member of the Altones, since 1950, when Al Winfield was the manager.

LeRoy Battle, now retired, resides in Harwood, Maryland, with his wife of 50 plus years, Alice, also a retired educator. His oldest son Terry, from his first marriage, is a professional musician who lives in Baltimore, Maryland. LeRoy and Alice have two children: Lisa, the oldest, is a medical doctor associated with Johns Hopkins Community Physicians in Baltimore, Maryland. LeRoy, Junior, is a professional musician who resides in Bowie, Maryland, with his wife Kimberly (Kim) and their three children, LeRoy III, Sydney, and Justice. LeRoy's mother and the matriarch of the family, Mrs. Marguerite (Margie) Goldwire Battle-Smith, was deceased in November 2006, after living to the age of 103 years young.

Contents

....

PART I

GROWING UP

My Lineage

My maternal grandmother, Isabelle Jones, who was born and raised in Augusta, Georgia, met my maternal grandfather, Henry Goldwire, at a Sunday School convention there. Henry Goldwire was from Clyo, a small, rural town in Georgia. It did not take long for a romance between the two of them to blossom. Isabelle and Henry married and made their first home in Clyo. Their first child, Roberta, was born there. However, Isabelle soon realized that she did not enjoy living in the country, so she and Henry moved to Savannah, Georgia. All of the other siblings were born there. In Savannah, grandfather Henry was a custodian at a large hotel. Grandmother Isabelle was a housewife. Born to Isabelle and Henry Goldwire after Roberta were six boys—namely William, Robert, Walter, Simpkin, Clarence, and Earl—with one more girl in between, Margie, my mother.

As soon as she was old enough, Roberta, the oldest, decided to go to Brooklyn, New York, to live. Once there, she enrolled in cosmetology school. Roberta passed the Brooklyn Board Examination and received her certificate from the Brooklyn School of Examiners, using the Apex System of Cosmetology. As soon as she was able to do so, Roberta opened up her own beauty parlor, which was also a cosmetology teaching school. She taught a large number of Negro females who wanted to become knowledgeable and efficient in the art of doing hair in the Apex Style. The alternate style was the Poro System. Both of these styles dealt with Negro females' hair dressing.

Very soon Roberta made it possible for the rest of her family to move to New York. Those moving included her parents, five of the six brothers, and her sister, Margie. One brother, Robby, decided not to go to New York. He stayed in Savannah and eventually became bell-captain at a leading hotel there.

The ages of the brothers when they moved to New York ranged from pre-teenager to young adults. Those who were old enough immediately found jobs, eventually making careers out of the occupations they enjoyed.

Their occupations were varied in nature. Grandfather Henry worked as the superintendent of a five-story apartment building located at 252 West 154th Street. William, the oldest of the brothers, became a mechanic and worked with the Montrose Pontiac dealership. He eventually lived in Amityville, Long Island, New York. Walter became an engineer and drove one of the subway trains on the Eighth Avenue Independent Line, eventually settling in Brooklyn. Clarence worked in the garment industry delivering suits, dresses, and the like. On the side he worked with the local politicians, garnering votes for them and arranging appointments with their constituents. He operated out of the local bars. During World War Two, Clarence was a merchant seaman. He was tall, a strapping six-foot, five inches, who possessed a deep, booming voice and was an avid cigar smoker.

Earl was the youngest of the brothers, in fact, of the siblings. He also became an engineer. He drove a train on the Brooklyn Eighth Avenue Independent Subway Line, also known as the "A" Train. Earl was only four years older than me. He was also tall, at six-foot, one inch, and had a smooth, tan complexion. Earl was also very fastidious about his attire, and wore his hair in the "fan" style. Fortunately, his sister was a hairdresser. With this style the front of the hairline was permitted to grow to a length of four or five inches, while the rest of the hair was cut relatively short. The fan was worn in three styles: standing straight up, slicked down, or wavy, and Earl chose a slight wave. Earl lived in Brooklyn.

During that time in New York City, one exciting and dangerous activity in which many of the young boys engaged was playing on the roofs of houses. One of the brothers, Simpkins, was playing on a roof, fell off, and died as a result of the fall. He was 14-years-old at the time.

Roberta Goldwire Roderick had a golden complexion, and a warm, full face with a ready smile. She was slightly heavier than my mother, dressed conservatively, and had an enviable work ethic. "Aunt Bert" was one of Brooklyn's very best hairdressers and, as stated, a teacher of aspiring beauticians.

The description of my mother during the time of my growing up is as follows: she possessed a beautiful full face with very expressive eyes, a lovely tan complexion, five-foot, eight inches tall, with a nice figure, strong, shapely legs, and weighing approximately 145 pounds. She always kept her hair in the latest style and was considered a "glamour girl." She had her clothes made to order by her favorite seamstress and she came upon the New York scene with a flair. She was called the "Queen" or the "Duchess" because of the outstanding, classy way she dressed. Mother eventually lived right around the corner from St. Mary's Catholic Hospital in Brooklyn. She would never fail to visit patients at the hospital, spreading God's words of joy. Many of the patients were neighborhood thugs who were recovering from knife or gunshot wounds. Mother would take them cool drinks. They had the highest respect for her. They would never use foul language in her presence and would not harm her in the streets. As she walked by, they would tip their caps and say to each other, "There goes the Duchess."

My father's family was from Rocky Mount, North Carolina. When my father moved to New York, his first order of business was to find a job. At first he did menial jobs at the Attentown House in Manhattan, New York. One day the manager of the variety shop in the lobby became ill, and the prognosis of the illness was that he would be out for quite some time. The owner of the hotel was pressed to secure the services of someone to operate the variety shop. Having observed my father in operation even doing the menial tasks, he garnered my father to take over during the illness of the previous manager.

After a period of time, the accountant and my father went over the books. They found that the profit had increased noticeably. The accountant was so impressed with this fact that he informed the owner. The owner was so pleased with this information that he rewarded my father with the management position of the variety shop on a permanent basis.

Margie Goldwire met her husband-to-be through his sister, Fannie Battle, in New York City. When they first married, my father Walter had already become manager of the variety shop in the lobby of the aforementioned hotel, so my mother became a housewife. His successful experiences with the variety shop gave him the courage to purchase his own candy store, and mother then became co-owner of the candy store. She subsequently became a caterer and also a premier beautician. My father, Walter Battle, was a medium height man, solidly built, with a dark brown complexion. He liked to wear caps and he was very strict.

I was the only child born to Margie and Walter Battle. During my early childhood, we lived at 269 West 154th Street. This was a family-oriented neighborhood, and it was very common for friends to eat at each others' homes unannounced. We had two policemen assigned to this area, which spanned from 145th Street up to 154th Street. Officer Dash was a Negro. His main responsibility was the youth gangs up to 14 years of age. Officer White was Caucasian, and his responsibility was the youth groups from ages 15 to young adults.

The candy store owned by my father was across the street from our apartment at 272 West 154th Street. There was a drug store on the corner, a grocery store, and a bar. At the drug store, whenever I got sick, my mother would send down for castor oil. The druggist would shake up a concoction of orange juice and the castor oil, but it would always separate by the time it got up to my home. The drink would separate unevenly, and the castor oil would always be on the top, so for a long period of time, oranges were not my favorite fruit.

The grocery store on the corner was very important, especially in the morning. The owner would have four or five steel milk barrels lined up against the wall. Each barrel would have a two-foot ladle that hooked on the outside of the can. When we came in with our pails, we would first remove the heavy round cover from the can, then take the ladle, dip the ladle in the can to get milk, and pour the milk into our pail to make one quart of milk. We would then replace the ladle inside the barrel to protect it from flies There was a hook on the handle of the ladle that would hang on the lip of the barrel when not in use. The heavy round cover would then be replaced on the barrel. Then we would go to the counter and pay 25 cents for the quart of milk. The area around the milk barrels was protected with fly paper hanging about five feet from the ceiling.

At night, the fathers would send their children to the bar with the same milk pails, this time to be filled with beer. The child would give the bartender a note and the money to pay for the beer. Then they would take the pail home to their father. Each bar had a "family" entrance. At that time there were no laws prohibiting children from entering bars for that particular purpose.

When I was young, any one of my uncles would take me to school. My uncles were Earl, Clarence, Walter, William, or Uncle Morales, who married my father's sister, Aunt Fannie. Uncle Morales would tell everyone that I was his son. He loved me very much. He taught me a lot of phrases in Spanish. My speaking knowledge of the Spanish language has served me in good stead. Even today I am quite comfortable speaking and understanding basic Spanish.

As a pre-teen, my errant ways usually reeked havoc with me. For example, when I was promoted to the fifth grade I wanted to show my classmates that I was the man. I ran my mouth and strutted like a ban-tam rooster. It wasn't long before my bluff was called. I was told by several of the boys to put up or shut up. I left the group with the following parting phrase, "I'll show you tomorrow."

That evening, my mother thought I was ill because I had hardly touched my favorite "meatball" supper. Instead, I had decided on what to do to prove to my classmates that I was the man. I waited in bed until both of my parents were asleep, then I quietly tiptoed into their room, crawled under their bed, and found the metal box in which my father kept his loose change from the candy store. I quietly raised the lid, reached in, grabbed a handful of coins, and retreated back to my room.

Now the lunch procedure at school was a follows: due to over-crowding and time restraints, sandwiches, cakes, pies, milk, and candy were wheeled around the school from room to room. Those students who did not "brown-bag" it could purchase food right there while sitting in their seats. After I arrived at school the next day, I informed a few of the boys that I was going to treat everyone in the class to a slice of pie or a candy bar. Each item cost five cents, and in no time at all, I was surrounded by my class members. I was gleefully handing out nickels while basking in the praise heaped on me by my "friends." To make a long story short, some of the girls told my teacher of their good fortune. My teacher investigated, then called my father. Well, between whacks from his leather belt on my naked behind and his preaching to me about the evils of right and wrong, I assured my father and anyone else who would listen that I would never, ever, do that again … and to this day I haven't.

Poor and Surviving in the "Cold Water" Flat

When I was approximately 11-years-old, my parents separated from each other. It is possible that I was partially aware of the difficulties that they were having, but the separation and subsequent divorce still came as a complete surprise to me. My lifestyle took a sudden turn for the worse. When Mother and I moved from Harlem to Brooklyn, we were very poor. Mother was a live-in maid and did not have an apartment. As a result I had to stay with my grandparents, Isabelle and Henry Goldwire, and my Uncle Earl. This move to my grandparents' apartment occurred during the early 1930s.

All through my adolescent years, everybody thought my grandparents were Jewish, because of their names, until people saw them. Grandmother Isabelle was dark-skinned and had a no-nonsense attitude. Grandfather Henry's complexion was café-au-lait. He was very easy going.

We lived in a "cold water" flat at 1616 Fulton Street, and our apartment was on the second floor. A cold water flat is an apartment without running hot water or steam heat. The only heat source was a coal burning stove in the kitchen, and the only way to get hot water was to heat a pan of water on the stove.

Once you unlocked the front door, you were greeted by a long hallway. One bedroom was on the left followed by a toilet. One bare bulb hanging from a four-foot cord was the hall light. At the end of the hall, you were met by two doors; each swung out towards you. The door on the left led into the kitchen, which was where we gathered for breakfast. The kitchen included a wood stove, four chairs, a table, an ice box, and a window box where, because of the cold, we could store perishable odds and ends.

The other door on the right opened into what we called the front room. There we would gather around the large Atwater-Kent radio and listen to the "Lone Ranger," the "Witch's Tales," "Amos and Andy," "Lowell Thomas and the Evening News." Mr. Thomas had a unique style that seemed to make the news come alive. I distinctly recall when he went to Tibet to see the Dalai Lama. Another of my favorites was the "Easy Aces," a show that centered around two folksy people and their quaint views on the events and the people in the community. The front room was our favorite family gathering place. Kerosene heaters were placed in the middle of the floor, and the door to the kitchen was left wide open so that the heat from the coal stove in the kitchen could also be felt. In the front room there was a broken piano, a davenport lounge (sofa and bed) that pulled out, and a small wooden table that held our schoolbooks and the newspaper. Grandma would have us clear the table to do our homework.

My Uncle Earl and I had to sleep in the hall bedroom and, boy, it was freezing there during the winter. Earl and I took turns heating the flat iron on the kitchen stove, and then we would quickly run to the hall bedroom and place the warm iron between the sheets. After three or four trips, we would dash to our room, set a record time changing in to our pajamas, jump into bed, then pull as much of the blankets up around our necks as possible so that no air could get in. Wintertime was the very hardest for those of us who were raised in cold water flats.

Grandmother was very strict with me, and my "devil-may-care" attitude would always clash with what she expected of me. As a result my tender backside would pay dearly for my hard head. Tears did not have any softening effect on Grandmother Isabelle. She would bellow to me, "Crying don't make it any better. The more you cry the less you 'pee'."

Getting Coal and Relief Food

It was very hard getting coal for our cold water flat. Small bags of coal were very heavy and costly. I used to hate it when grandmother would get a few empty gunnysacks. Once or twice a week we would walk to Eastern Parkway, pulling a small wagon. This was where the wealthy Jewish people lived. There we would go to the approximately 15 ash cans lined up in a row that the building janitor had set out. We would scrounge through each can looking for unburned lumps of coal. It would take us about an hour to fill our sacks, and then we would head for home pulling our heavy load.

Another routine that I disliked was going with my grandmother to the Central Relief Center in our neighborhood. There we would join a slow moving line of people. When we reached each window, we would take a can of food or a bag of flour. By the time we reached the last window, our sack would be filled with canned beef, flour, canned milk, corn meal, canned vegetables, etc. One could always tell the relief food because of the white labels and dark blue letters on the containers. On occasion they would also give us butter. I felt embarrassed for others in the neighborhood to see me. Little did I realize that we were all in the same socioeconomic class of "have-nots."

A Night Visitor

Early one morning, I got the scare of my life. It must have been around three AM. I heard a sound like someone was lapping water. I went into the bathroom and switched on the light. A scream froze in my throat. There protruding from the commode were the back and long tail of a huge gray rat. Our toilet bowl was the funnel type (some had a flat ledge). The rat was trying to back up and out. He had evidently tried to get a drink of water, but his weight took him all the way in until he became stuck.

As the rat struggled to get out, it made so much noise that I awakened my Uncle Earl out of fear, grabbing a broomstick at the same time. He said to me, "What are you going to do with that broomstick?"

"I'm going to beat him to death," I replied.

"No," Earl said. "He might get out, and a wounded, cornered rat is the worst thing you could face." Finally Earl said, "Get the foot tub, fill it with water, and let it boil on the stove."

After about 30 minutes, we took the boiling water, mixed it with soap powder, then took care of the rat. Grandpa said we did very well, and he then disposed of our night visitor.

Uncle Tom

In the mid-1930s, there was a very, very popular program that used to be broadcast over the radio called "Uncle Tom." The format of this long-running series revolved around the adventures of a middle-aged gentleman and his teenage niece and nephew. They lived and traveled in a Land Cruiser. Today we would call this a recreational vehicle. It boggled our young minds to hear about the adventures of this group as they traveled each week from city to city.

One week they picked up a hitchhiker who turned out to be an escaped convict. Another week they encountered a lady who was alone on the road at midnight. The lady was crying and stated that the couple at the place where she was staying had put her out because she couldn't pay the rent. However, they had kept her baby and would not give it to her.

Another episode involved a group of teenage boys who were vandalizing the cars where the Land Cruiser had parked to spend the night. The nephew heard a loud crash. He then looked out of the window by his bed and saw several teenage boys breaking car windows with baseball bats. The nephew awakened Uncle Tom and told him quickly what was happening. Uncle Tom sprang into action immediately. He opened the door and yelled, "Police, Police. Help!" This startled the vandals and they scattered, but not before Uncle Tom and his nephew caught two of the gang.

To say that "Uncle Tom" was popular with the general public, both children and adults, is putting it mildly. In fact, one could readily compare his popularity with that of with Pick Temple, Howdy Doody, or Mr. Rogers.

It distresses me to have to tell the sad ending to Uncle Tom's program. Usually after the theme song was played, which signaled the end of the show, the broadcast engineer would hit a switch that told the performers that they were "off-the-air" and the microphone was turned off. On this particular evening, however, the engineer failed to shut the microphone off and a very relaxed "Uncle Tom" was heard to say for all of the radio audience to hear, "There, that ought to hold the little bastards." There was an immediate "Hue and Cry," which resulted in the "Uncle Tom" program being taken off the air.

Significant Adults While Growing Up

I Remember Duke Ellington

The Duke made a lasting impression on me ever since I started on my way to becoming a professional musician.

I recall my mother going to dances and cabarets whenever the Ellington band was playing. Mother would get on the phone, call her best friend Ethel Cleveland, and the both of them would spend literally an hour planning what they were going to wear and how their hair would be fixed (mother always cut her hair in the "pageboy" style when she would attend dances requiring evening dresses, etc.). On this particular Saturday, the Duke Ellington Orchestra was to play at the Audubon Ballroom (the Audubon was a very popular dance hall rented by the elite Colored social clubs.)

After Mother and Mrs. Cleveland left for the cabaret, I called my best friend Walter Williams and said to him, "Dickie, I've just got to go to the Audubon to see the Duke." I really wanted to check out his great drummer, Sonny Greer. I had all of the records by Duke and, as a beginning jazz drummer, I loved Sonny's tom-tom playing on "Caravan" and also his fast beat on "Cottontail."

Dickie had a beat up "tin lizzie," so we finally got to the Audubon. Now we were minors, so we had to be very smart to sneak in, which we did through a basement window. As we entered the dark room, we had to pause for a few minutes to allow our eyes to get used to the dark. After a while, we could see the staircase leading upstairs to the dance floor. We had to navigate around pianos, drum sets, and lots of tables and chairs. Finally, we eased our way up to the door leading to the marvelous sounds of the orchestra. I could hardly keep my composure because of those thrilling drum throbs coming through the door.

We gently cracked the door and were met by heavy stage curtains. We eased up, lightly pulled back the curtain, and the sight was like a picture out of Hollywood.

We were in back of the band, which was set up on tiers. The drummer, Sonny Greer, was set up on the top tier. Sonny was surrounded by full orchestra chimes and he was playing his part to Duke's "Ring Dem Bells." His drummer's throne was in the middle of four timpani (painted white and in different sizes). There were his bass drum foot pedal and floor tom-toms to one side, and cymbals and snare drum to the other.

The next tier down had trombones and trumpets, followed by a lower tier of woodwinds (saxes and clarinets). In the middle floor level was Duke, seated at a small white baby grand piano. All the musicians were dressed in white tails.

The stage manager came up to us and said in a not-too-friendly voice, "You boys come here now!"

Well, I whispered to Dickie, "Let me talk." As we approached the stage manager, I spoke in a pleading voice, "Please mister, all we want to do is to meet the greatest orchestra leader of them all—the great Duke."

The stage manager looked at us and, just at that time, the orchestra was going on a short break. I could hear Duke telling the people, "Love ya madly. We'll be right back." The stage manager signaled us to stay put. He went out onto the stage and, in a few seconds, he and Duke appeared before us.

"What're your names?" he asked.

I spoke for both of us, saying, "My name is Boots, sir, and this is my best friend, Dickie. I play drums in a 15-piece band, and I just had to see you and Sonny Greer."

With that, Duke called out loud to Sonny, beckoned him over, and made my life complete! I might add that, to this day, I insist that any band I lead must wear tuxedos.

The Black Eagle of Harlem

It was in the middle 1930s that I became aware of a man of mystery who was a legend in his own time; his name was Hubert Julian, Colonel Hubert Julian, to be exact. He measured about five feet nine inches in height, had a brown, swarthy complexion, and short, wavy hair, parted in the middle. He sported a short, clipped mustache that framed a ready smile that exposed even white teeth. He had slight dimples in each cheek and his eyes were very piercing and jet black; one could imagine "snake eyes." He would always come into my father's candy store around noon to pick up the afternoon paper, *The Mirror.*

I was always in awe of the way he dressed—he wore a jet black double-breasted jacket with white pearl buttons on both sides. At his throat was a white silk cravat adorned with a jet-black pearl in the middle. His trousers were a banker's gray color with delicate black vertical stripes. His pumps were black with off-white spats. He always wore thin, light gray patent leather gloves. On his head he sported a light gray Homburg. In his right eye he had a monocle, which was attached by a silver chain to his lapel. (I was always fascinated to see the monocle fall from his eye when he and my father enjoyed a joke.) Completing his outfit was a silver-tipped walking cane, which he used to hail a cab or to point to an object on the shelf behind my father.

One day Colonel Julian was regaling my dad and about five other customers with his stories of adventures and flying. I later learned that he was a colonel in Haile Salassie's Air Force, which consisted of no more than one patched-up and shot-up single engine plane. I do know that Colonel Julian had connections in Washington, DC. I recall one evening he was involved in a heated discussion in my father's store. Colonel Julian held up both hands and said, "All right, I'll show you." With that statement, he pulled a thick leather pouch from his inside pocket and said, "Read this." Then, with a flourish, he opened the pouch and a stack of attached five- by seven-inch cards tumbled out like an accordion, unfolding until they touched the floor. Some cards were light blue, some were pink, and some were white.

Each card was adorned with the figure of blind justice in the background, and imprinted with the following statement, "The bearer of this card has permission to enter the various rooms or chambers in which hearings are being held." Everyone in the store looked stunned. There was a sly smirk on Colonel Julian's face as he gathered up the cards, inserted the pouch inside his walking coat jacket, placed the monocle in his eye socket, turned with a slight head bow as he touched the tip of his cane to his Homburg brim, clicked his heels, and said in a forceful voice, "Auf-wiedersehen."

That was the last I saw or heard from the Black Eagle until one day at chow, when I was a Tuskegee Aviation cadet. As we were filing out of the mess hall, emptying our trays, there on the large bulletin board was a large 12- by 15-inch black and white glossy picture of Colonel Hubert Julian standing beside his old fighter plane. He was dressed with flying helmet, goggles, pilot jacket, and white scarf. The large caption on the photo said, "Colonel Hubert Julian Challenges Reich Marshall Hermann Goering to a one-on-one duel over the Atlantic." He sent the photo and the challenge to the Third Reich, but there was no response.

Buck and Bubbles

154th Street and Eighth Avenue was a very busy and thriving block. As I look back on those times I realize that it was a middle-class block. Colonel B. O. Davis, Sr., who later became the first Black General in the United States Army, resided there, along with the famous Black song-and-dance team, Buck and Bubbles. Buck, who was tall and slim, would do the various forms of dancing—tap, shimmy, the big apple, and all of the other dances done in every Negro house at that time. Bubbles was short and squatty. He always sat and played the piano during the act. Bubbles would always wear a very large, garishly-colored cap, and Buck always wore a derby. Bubbles delivered the punch lines during their repartee. I recall seeing one show where Bubbles was at the piano on the extreme right side of the stage, and Buck was at a microphone on the extreme left. At one point, Buck said to Bubbles, "I got a good mind to come over there and go upsides your big head."[1]

To which Bubbles replied, "First of all, I wouldn't call that a good mind! And, second of all, while I can't stop you from comin' over here, I can sure delay your departure!"

Buck and Bubbles were very important in my life because they inspired me to become an entertainer. When they returned from their road trips (they were booked from New York to California), they would come to my father's candy store and treat everyone there to Whistle orange soda, Eskimo pies, and cake. It was a joy for me to listen as they regaled us with what had happened during their exciting engagements.

The Dean Dixon Story

As a postscript to the Dean Dixon story,[2] let me add the following. In spite of the fact that Mr. Dixon was one of the best, if not *the* best, conductor in America, the racist policy pervading our culture kept him down. He could not get sponsors to back an orchestra. He did not

---

[1] **Author's Note**: *For a prior reference to Buck and Bubbles, look at page five in my first book,* Easier Said, *beginning with line six in paragraph two.*

receive the recognition of being a regular guest conductor with the elite orchestras in New York City; namely, the Philharmonic Orchestra or the NBC Symphonic Orchestras. Consequently, Dean Dixon went to Europe where he soon became the toast of the continent.

Early Work Experiences

Elevator Operator

From the time that I was 14, I worked at many jobs, but I always had my drumsticks nearby. I recall being employed as an elevator operator at the famous St. George's Hotel in Brooklyn. I looked pretty spiffy in my dress uniform, which consisted of a white shirt, dark brown knitted tie, tan suit coat trimmed in white with brown lapels, a silver lanyard cord around my left shoulder, and dark brown trousers with white side piping. All this was topped off with brown socks and shoes.

The day I applied, the bell captain had me ride with him all morning. The toughest part was stopping the elevator evenly with each floor so that the passengers would not trip. Such an accident could result in a very expensive lawsuit for the hotel. After lunch, which we ate for free in a special room designated for the employees, the bell captain said, "Battle, go get changed and take over the Tower Elevator, number three." Now, the Tower Elevator was just what the name implied. The regular elevators could go only as high as the 15th floor. The Tower Elevator was special and could go up to the 22nd floor. Persons residing in the Tower were very well off. They had permanent apartments and were treated in a special way. The elevator made express stops only from the first floor to the 16th floor and above. After a week, I was assigned to night duty. I liked this because the patrons would always tip

[2] **Author's Note**: *Please refer to page 42 in my first book,* Easier Said, *the first paragraph, beginning with line 10.*

me as they egressed. One night I noticed quite a bit of activity going on in a certain apartment on the 19th floor. Waiters were carrying trays laden with glasses and intoxicating beverages in and out. Beautiful ladies who looked like movie stars were frequenting the apartment.

Finally I asked the bell captain what was going on. He told me to keep quiet and just operate my Otis elevator. Finally, I caught on. It was "love for sale." About two AM, a man got on the elevator and whispered to me, "Where's the action, Sonny?"

I replied, "Things seem to be lively in 1973."

He pressed a 20-dollar bill in my hand as he got off on 19. That was quite a learning experience for me.

At Floyd Bennett Airfield

During the summer of 1938, I was 17 and I would read the classified section of the *Daily News* and the *Daily Mirror*, vainly looking for employment opportunities. One evening I saw an ad announcing job openings in the officers' mess at Floyd Bennett Airfield in the flatlands of Brooklyn, New York. Positions were available for waiters, table setters, dishwashers, breakdown and cleanup porters, etc. The pay would vary; however, no salary would be lower than 25 dollars a week.

The next morning I called the personnel office of Floyd Bennett Airfield. The manager explained to me that the job entailed living in six nights a week, with the workday starting at six AM and ending at four PM. He then asked me if I could start that very day. I told him that I had to check with my mother, and then I would call him back as soon as possible. When I told Mother what had transpired, she was quite proud of the fact that I had taken the initiative to seek out and land a job. I immediately called the manager, who then gave me directions on how to get there.

The next 15 minutes were spent cramming the clothes I figured I would need for a week into a suitcase. In the background, Mother was warning me about fast women, smoking, etc. I kissed Mother goodbye and went to the subway. After changing trains a few times, I arrived at the Floyd Bennett stop. There I had to board an airfield bus. Unfortunately, the road leading to the entrance gate was being resurfaced, so I had to exit the bus and lug my ragged suitcase for over a quarter of a mile to the entrance gate. The spiffy military policeman—with starched, razor-sharp creases in his outfit—directed me to a hangar that was another 100 yards to my right. This time the walk did not seem so long. I stopped a few times just to view the "Yellow Perils" taking off and landing. All of the Navy training airplanes were bi-winged and painted a bright yellow. It was a thrill to view the pilots, and one even waved to me.

I finally arrived at the hangar and went through a large opening, where a sign directed me to the office. A female clerk checked me in, gave me papers to sign, and called the kitchen to send someone up. Soon a man came in and beckoned, "Follow me."

In a few minutes I was ushered into a large room that was lined on both sides with double-decker beds. One of the stewards extended his hand and said, "Welcome, we're sure glad to see you. We're quite short of hands. You'll sleep here in the upper bunk and you can store your clothes in that empty locker. Wash up and change. You are going to be the busboy at today's luncheon. The pilots have been flying for over four hours and they are going to be starved."

I quickly washed and changed into a white mess jacket and trousers with small black and gray checks. The steward took me to the officers' mess. It was a cozy, well-furnished room with a long, wide, old English table around which were about 20 heavy, mahogany tall-back chairs with padded leather seats. The walls were filled with engraved pictures depicting flying activities, along with one long mural showing an aerial dogfight. Soon soft music was piped in, and then I heard them, the flyers. They were all cocky white boys, full of themselves.

Instructors were telling some flyers about the mistakes they had made; they were demonstrating with both hands, emulating dives and splits. The waiters came in with plates steaming with steaks, etc. Boy, I was so hungry; I had not eaten since six AM. I was kept hopping, first filling the glasses and then refilling them with iced tea, going to the kitchen for more rolls, and later bringing out the iced water and ice cream.

Finally, after the flyers left, a big fat man wearing a large chef's hat and apron opened the doors, motioned to me, and said, "C'mon rookie, it's time for us to eat." There in the corner of the kitchen, around a small, round table, we sat down to eat. Man, I was ready for one or two of those broiled steaks. You could have knocked me over with a feather when the chef uncovered a plate of baloney sandwiches, coffee, and Jell-O; not the steak and the pie a la mode I had served the flyers. The chef must have read the look of disappointment on my face. He scowled at me saying, "Eat, boy, and be quick about it. You've got to clear those dishes from the dinner meal and set up for supper." Right then I had second thoughts about the job.

Around 4:30 PM, one of the stewards said, "You did pretty good, considering. C'mon. Let's make tracks for the hangar."

I saw that all of the bunks were occupied with Negroes—some reading, some playing cards, and a radio on a chair was tuned to a blues station. These were all older men who did not pay me any mind. As I climbed up to my bunk and stretched out (I was tired), I heard soft laughter, with the tone that told you that something was going on at your expense. I turned my head and looked in the direction of the laughter, and then all got quiet.

Entering the room was this tremendously fat chef. He ambled over to the group, wheezing as he moved, sat down with a thump and a grunt, and said something to the men in the group. Then they all looked at me and someone said, to no one in particular, but for all to hear, "Yes sir, Chef is going to sample some new meat tonight." A chill went right through me. I was young, but I was no neophyte; my life in the New York streets had taught me a thing or two. I made up my mind right then and there that this job was for the birds.

My solution to this problem was quite simple. At one AM, when all were asleep, I located my suitcase—which luckily I had not unpacked —changed my clothes, and left the hangar. I literally ran the distance to the subway and, around four AM, I rang the doorbell of my "Home Sweet Home."

A Riot in Harlem

On the weekend of March 19, 1935, the musical combo in which I was drumming had just finished playing a gig at the Triangle Inn, located in Quogue, Long Island, New York. During breakfast, we nervously talked about the unrest voiced by certain political activist groups based in Harlem. They were agitated about the lack of jobs for Negro people, empty stomachs, overcrowded tenements, filthy sanitation, rotten food stuffs, chiseling absentee landlords, and police brutality.

As we loaded our instruments onto the train, which was to carry us to Grand Central Station in Manhattan, one of the redcaps pulled me aside and warned me to be very careful because there was a riot going on in the heart of 125th Street, our destination. Needless to say, our band was very much on edge as we rode to the city; the passengers were visibly upset and eyed us askance and with apprehension. In return, seeing that the members of our band were the only people of color in the coach, we assumed a feigned air of nonchalance, discussing our next upcoming gig and its ramifications.

As we neared Grand Central Station, a conductor came to our coach and announced that there was a disturbance going on quite close to the station. As we egressed, the scene that greeted us was one of hustle, bustle, and complete chaos. Policemen, both mounted and on foot, were everywhere. We were very fortunate to get a cab driven by a Negro man, because several cabs driven by Whites had refused to pick us up.

As we approached Seventh Avenue and 125th Street, we viewed crowds breaking windows and looting. The driver told us that all stores owned by Negro people were left intact, while windows of White store-owners were being smashed and the merchandise taken. As we continued driving into the fray, I saw a sign that spoke volumes, even though it was one simple declarative statement. It was in the window of a Chinese laundry; in large, black, block letters on white cardboard, it read: "ME COLORED TOO!" That sign proved to be effective, because the next day I read that the Chinese laundry was not vandalized.

Very recently, I received a letter from the New York Historical Society regarding the above riot. The letter was from Mr. Eric Robinson, reference assistant, and states as follows: "The riot you discussed in your book is referred to as the Kress Riot, which occurred on March 19, 1935, as written up in *The Black New Yorkers—The Schomberg Illustrated Chronology*."

March 19, 1935

Long-simmering charges of police brutality boil over when Lino Rivera, a black high school student, is arrested for allegedly stealing a pocketknife at the S.H. Kress Five and Dime Store on 125th Street in Harlem. False rumors spread that Rivera had been beaten to death by police. By nightfall, more than 10,000 angry black residents are protesting in the 125th Street main shopping area. Some in the crowd break the windows of white-owned businesses and rampage through the streets. Five hundred police and white merchants demanded that Governor Herbert Lehman send in the National Guard. Lehman refuses. About 200 stores are destroyed, with property losses of over two million dollars. A hundred blacks are arrested, three are killed, and 30 more are injured.

Most historians agree that the "Kress Riot" of 1935 had a chilling effect, ending the Harlem Renaissance that began circa 1921 (the year of my birth).

Cross the Burning Sands

I attended Morgan State College in Baltimore, Maryland in 1946. I was 25-years-old at the time and wanted to join the fraternity Omega Psi Phi. Saturdays, usually a day to look forward to for most college students, was a day of "terror for us lamps."

On this particular Saturday, five of us pledges were selected to stand in front of the local theatre for a period of six hours, starting at 11 AM. This, in itself, was bad enough. However, we were required to drape a white sheet over our clothes, like the ancient Greeks. In our left hand we carried three textbooks. In our right hand we carried a light bulb. We were lined up about 10 feet apart. At the stroke of 11, we had to raise the hand that held the bulb and shout, "A mind must be fed with words and light." We then had to count to 25 silently and repeat the sentence over and over.

They did give us 15 minutes to wolf down a hamburger and soda. As the patrons entered the theater, they would ask us all types of questions, take our pictures, and exclaim, "How can they treat you so cruelly?" We could not even acknowledge their presence. At the end of our time, a van would appear, driven by an upper classmate, and pick us up. This part of the ritual was designed to teach us humility and endurance.

The night before we "crossed over"—that is, going from a neophyte to a full-fledged Q or Omega Man—we were assembled around midnight, loaded into several cars, and driven to different locations. There were two other neophytes in the car with me. We were blindfolded before we got in the car. To disorient us, we were driven around in circles before the driver set out to their destination. About 20 minutes later, the cars stopped, we were put out, and then told to count to 25 before removing our blindfolds. The task at hand was to get back to Morgan before daybreak. If they had to send a car to pick any of us up, all of us would be dropped from the rolls. This would be a shameful thing to face if we were banned, so we each silently vowed to think and act together.

We removed our blindfolds. Boy, it was dark. We couldn't see our hands in front of our faces. We got our bearings by looking up and checking the top of the trees against the sky. Finally, after several false starts, we decided upon the direction we wanted to go. It was about four AM, and we were starting to become concerned that we wouldn't meet our deadline. Traffic was very light, so we could not zero in, for sure, on the direction of the main boulevard.

We were exhausted, tired, and hungry. The situation looked hopeless. Then, just before we were willing to plop down and await the ultimate humiliation, we heard the sweetest sound this side of heaven. It was the wail of the siren on a fire truck. Then we heard the rumble of the hook and ladder. We didn't know where it was headed but we knew where the firehouse was and, without a moment's hesitation, we struck out in the direction that would take us to the road home. Once we arrived at the reservoir, we basically knew where we were. We sat down, took our shoes off, shook the dollar bills out of our shoes (we had hidden the money in case we needed some), and prayed for a taxi.

We were laughing and talking as we walked, attempting to keep each other's spirits up because of our race against time. At one point we saw a pair of very bright headlights heading our way. One of us yelled, "Hey, over here!" Well, we could have been knocked over with a feather when all of a sudden the car was enveloped with red and white flashing lights.

The squad car pulled up beside us and I immediately started explaining to the officers who we were, what we were doing at the reservoir, and the pickle we were in because we couldn't find a cab. Both policemen, one Negro and one White, started laughing. Then they said, "Hop in boys. You're in luck."

So we piled in the back, very thankful for this unexpected help. We had no sooner started on our way when one of the neophytes said to no one in particular, "Boy, I'm hungry. Even when we get to Morgan we won't be able to buy anything."

At that, the car took a sudden turn and we looked at each other and hunched our shoulders. Soon I recognized North Avenue and, within a few minutes, the car pulled with a jerk in front of Nate's and Leon's, the most celebrated delicatessen in Baltimore. Nate's, as we called it for short, was famous for its smoked turkey, tuna, roast beef, strawberry short cake, etc. One of the policemen said, "Order take out, fellows."

The policemen treated us, then took us all the way to Morgan. We thanked them profusely. They laughed, winked, then waved so long to us, saying, "Get some good grades. We could use some help." As they drove away, I thought of a saying I had heard somewhere: "Be grateful. You'll never know from whence comes your help."

Well, we ran into one of the neophyte's room, cleared a desk, spread the food out, and said down to a veritable feast. Just then, an upperclassman came into the room and said, "Dogs, who gave you permission to eat?"

Without blinking, I said, "The President did, sir."

He said, "Okay," took a chicken wing, and left.

We neophytes looked at each other and smiled. Then I said, "That's a small price to pay for a moment's peace." We shut the door, ate, then fell asleep where we sat, content with the knowledge that come daylight we would be full-fledged Omega men.

1950s Life

Archery Trip and Tournament

It was in fall 1951 that I was explaining to a captive audience, which included Wilbur Tolson and Ruth and Ben Cumbo, the details of my Archery Club's upcoming trip to Clifton Forge, Virginia, to take part in a Field Archery Tournament to be held the next Sunday.

I was truly wound up and excited about this event, and had succeeded in so heightening the interest of those present that they exclaimed they wanted to accompany me there to observe my club, The Mohican Bowman, in action. I told them they had to dress warmly and wear jackets and pants that would hug their wrists and ankles (to keep out ticks and mites). They were advised to pack sandwiches, water, and plenty of hot coffee, and chocolate candy (for energy).

Sunday rolled around and part of the club rode in the lead car and I went with Wilbur, et al., in the other car. The trip was long but the scenery was beautiful; the autumn leaves could best be described as God's bouquet. As far as one's eye could behold, there was a riotous panorama of colors, including lime, raspberry, purple, orange, etc. The trees were showing off their most enviable tints.

After four hours (we had left Upper Marlboro, Maryland, at five AM), we pulled into a very quiet Clifton Forge. We were surrounded by mountains, hills, and gullies. To our right we saw the Clifton Forge Veterans' Administration Hospital, with tall chimneys that belched out smoke over a very crowded parking area.

We motored slowly along the main street, seeking directions to the archery range. Wilbur said, "Boots, there is a diner over there to our left; let's go in and order breakfast."

Ruth replied, "Yes, and I would like to freshen up; this has been a long ride."

I immediately pulled into a parking space directly in front of the diner. Passengers in both cars piled out, and I said, "We're a few minutes late, so just make this a 'pit stop' with coffee. We will chow down later." I told them to watch their bows (strung) and holster their arrows so that we would be ready when we hit the range.

A few seconds later, we entered the diner. There were a couple of white hunters at a nearby table eating breakfast. They both stopped chewing their chow and glared at us with wide-open eyes. We must have presented quite a formidable picture: black archers with strung bows, hunting knives at our side, and our quivers filled with target-destroying arrows.

I told the others to be seated at the counter and tables, and to be sure to order a coffee and a doughnut for me. I then went directly to where the two men were sitting, gave them my most charming smile, and asked for directions to the Clifton Forge Archery Range. Without smiling, one of the diners got up and, in a thick, Appalachian brogue, told me to wait there while he made his way to the wall phone. I couldn't hear what he was saying, so I wandered to the counter, where I saw an elderly black man with a spotty apron (from washing dishes) talking with Ruth and the others. As I approached, I heard him exclaim, "Just where are you folks from? They never allow people of our color to come in here. They almost beat a Black man to death last year for daring to sit at this very counter." He showed fear and cringed a little as he took in what I'm certain he viewed as our "battle weapons."

Just then, two white men entered the diner, one dressed with white shirt and tie, and the other with olive fatigues and a hunting knife at his side. He gave us a warm greeting and introduced himself as Dr. Ambruse, President of the Clifton Forge Archery Club. He then turned to the owner of the diner and said, "I think these folks could use some coffee and coffee cake, Jim."

He then turned to me and asked what state we were from. He was very impressed when I told him. After awhile, the doctor asked us to load up and follow him to the range. We knew the routine. First, report to the Tournament Director, have our equipment examined, pay our entry fees, and get classified to go with our appropriate shooting average group. Then go to the practice range to warm up.

Needless to say, there was a lot of interest exhibited by the white archers toward us. All of our practice shots were in the target face or the bale. None of our arrows went awry by missing the entire bale, as we knew that would prove to be very embarrassing.

At the end of the contest, I'm proud to say that I took first place in the archer's category with an average score of 173. I still have the Gold Ash Tray (First Place) at my home on my mantelpiece.

The Mohican Bowmen's participation in the Clifton Forge Archers Tournament was a resounding success. I have to laugh when I think of Ben Cumbo (my best friend, who was a physical education teacher at the Frederick Douglass Elementary Junior Senior High School in Upper Marlboro, Maryland), shivering in his seersucker pants due to the cold autumn wind, because he had ignored my advice to dress warmly. Be not alarmed, however, because Ben and Wilbur found a means to warm their insides thoroughly.

I was very happy to learn from Wilbur later that, after enrolling at West Virginia State College, he took up archery as a result of his trip with me to Clifton Forge, and became quite adept with the bow and arrow. I am also convinced that it was Ruth Cumbo's radiant smile and personality that "defanged" those hostile eyes and stares at us.

Bow Hunting Trip to West Virginia

One of the most harrowing, difficult experiences I ever had with bow hunting occurred just before Labor Day in 1952. At that time, Al

Winfield and I headed for the border of West Virginia, just east of Martinsburgh, Virginia.

We drove his bright blue Nash as far up the mountains as the terrain would allow. All of a sudden, through the ground fog, we observed about 30 wild turkeys eating their way up the mountainside. As luck would have it, our bows were unstrung and in the trunk of the car.

We unlatched the door and tried to be as quiet as possible. All of a sudden, a voice, thick with the mountain twang, yelled out, "You boys got your permit to hunt this year?" We turned to see a very fat park ranger with an Army .45 hanging below his stomach.

"Yessir," we gingerly answered as we turned around for him to see and examine the licenses pinned to our backs. The ranger then spit a mouthful of tobacco juice that seemed to spray over him before it hit the ground. He said, "Okay boys, I'll show you a good spot to get 'on stand' while you're hunting deer."

We followed him for about 100 yards until we came upon a small, rustic log cabin next to a very high "lookout" tower. He said, "Here's where I live for three months at a time. A relief ranger will take over in December. Go in and take a look-see."

We opened the log cabin door and were greeted by a strange sight. There was an army cot against one wall, surrounded by shelves and shelves of canned food; there must have been over 100 cans of corned beef, sardines, peaches, etc., and another shelf had boxes and boxes of crackers. "This is the fare we live off during our stay," he said. "If we want coffee, we build a fire outside, and boil it the old-fashioned way."

He then suggested we climb to the top of the lookout tower. After what seemed like a lifetime, we hauled ourselves to the top platform, which was glass enclosed. We used his powerful binoculars to check in all directions. "You can see close to 30 miles on a clear day, so it is very easy to spot smoke. I use this crystal combination radio to communicate with other stations." By this time it was getting dark, so we climbed down. The ranger told us to sleep in the car and not to wander around in the dark.

The next morning, Al and I heard a tapping on the car window. It was the ranger holding a pot of coffee and three cups. I never had coffee without cream and sugar before; however, we were freezing and that cup of black coffee was the best ever and seemed to take the chills right out of my body.

We repaid the ranger for his kindness by sharing the slab bacon we brought along. We also opened a can of baked beans and had quite a meal. Later, we thanked him and drove off in the direction of where the deer were supposed to be. All of a sudden a very heavy fog rolled in—we really could not see the hood of the car. This bode heavy trouble for us because, for about 50 yards, we only had space the width of the car to negotiate. We turned on the headlights and Al said, "Boots, you steer while I walk in front to guide you." I could sense where Al was (he had a flashlight that he waved back and forth), and we kept the pace of five miles an hour for 20 minutes. Finally, we broke into a broad, flat area. We decided to camp there for the night. The next morning, the fog was still with us and as I emerged from the car, I saw a sight that made me swallow very hard. There, all around our car, were huge bear paw prints, and here and there were bear droppings as large as an eight-inch plate.

We enclosed ourselves in the car and ate crackers and summer sausage, accompanied by bear howls in the background. The fog finally lifted the next day by noon. Very thankfully our hunting trip came to an end and, no, we did not bag any deer.

How I Met Alice

Several readers of my autobiography, *Easier Said*, were interested in how I met my wife, Alice. It was a lovely day in the fall of October 1956. At the time, I was teaching at the Frederick Douglass Elementary Junior Senior High School in Upper Marlboro, Maryland.

I had just finished rehearsing our marching band after school. It seems that Mr. Frisby, our principal, had called for an emergency Parent Teacher Association (PTA) meeting (for some reason, I did not get the announcement.)

Our band practice was over at six PM. I was ready to catch a ride home when our guidance counselor, Miss Thelma Daly, saw me in the hall and said, "Boots, where do you think you're going?"

"Home," I replied.

"Aren't you forgetting that the PTA meets tonight?"

"Good grief," I replied. "I can't go back to my apartment and return to school in time. Well," I continued, "I'll just have to eat some candy and make do." (Upper Marlboro was fiercely segregated and people of color did not have any place to dine, etc.)

Thelma said, "That's okay, Boots, I've been invited to my friend Alice Holt's house for dinner—she will not mind if you come along."

Well, I hopped into Thelma's car and we drove across the bridge to Wayson's Corner, and turned left onto "Sands Road;" it was honestly named. A short while later, we pulled up into the yard of a quaint two-story, white-shingled colonial.

I followed Thelma onto the porch, where a beautiful brown-skinned angel was conversing with a genteel, lovely elderly couple. Thelma and this angelic person greeted each other with hugs and I was introduced all around. My heart skipped a beat when the angel looked me directly in the eye, extended a hand of friendship, and said, "Hello Roy, I'm Alice."

The rest is history; I had to pass "muster" for Alice's parents, her five brothers, two sisters, and countless nieces and nephews. By the way, that was my first honest-to-goodness country dinner; everything was homegrown or homemade: country ham, collard greens (a broad-leaf green, similar to kale), corn bread, mashed potatoes, iced tea, apple dumplings. That was one Parent Teacher Association meeting where I was truly a "happy camper."

Study and Practice

While some people seem to search their whole lives to discover who they are and what they want to be, I was fortunate. The first time I saw a marching band, I fell in love with the uniforms and music. This love grew as I watched the Color Guard at school assemblies. As I listened to the drum cadence to which they marched, I knew I wanted to be a drummer and member of the Color Guard.

We had no money for drums, so my mother's pots and pans became my means of practice. Then I was able to use an old drum that belonged to the Boy Scouts. Finally, through the church finance committee, I got a set of new drums. The culmination of my practice—beginning with my mother's muffin tin to my own set of drums—was that I made the Color Guard. I had set a goal for myself, worked hard to accomplish it, and succeeded.

This experience stood me in good stead when I was hired as the music teacher for Douglass Elementary High School in Upper Marlboro because there was no music program there at that time. I began with the goal of establishing a music program, worked hard with the students and community, and finally succeeded in having one of the finest programs in the area.

However, the journey from Color Guard to Douglass High took a lot of years, a lot of study, and, most of all, a lot of practice. I learned early on that, without the disciplines of study and practice, I would never be the kind of drummer I wanted to be. I also learned that being a musician would affect all areas of my life. I spent my time practicing and playing with local bands rather than being on the streets. After the fulfillment I had found in working with others to create moments of excellence and beauty, the thought of robbing a person or a store couldn't hold a candle to the holistic magnificent chords of a Bach cantata.

Thus, as a music teacher, I was able to say to parents, "Let me teach your child to blow a horn and I promise you he'll never blow a safe."

My drumming skills also played a part in my Army career. When I was drafted during World War II, I volunteered to train as a Tuskegee Airman. My hours of drum practice had honed my hand-eye coordination skills to the point that I was the only one of the four in my group to pass the qualification test. It was through my drumming that I discovered my true vocation, being a teacher. I was still in junior high when I had my first two pupils. My first pupil, Ernie Stewart, offered to teach me swing in exchange for music reading lessons. My second pupil was the son of a white woman who my mother sometimes cooked for, and I got paid the exorbitant fee of seven dollars a week. From these experiences, I learned how gratifying it could be to pass your knowledge and skills on to someone else.

That feeling never left me. I played with several combos over the years and went to Juilliard after graduating from high school, but I never got over my desire to be a teacher. I transferred to Morgan State in Baltimore, got my degree, and started my teaching career at Douglass. As the program began to build, I worked hard to keep my promise to the parents that their children would learn more than how to play instruments, they would also learn dedication, self-discipline, self-confidence, and self-esteem. Perhaps most importantly, they would learn to work together and depend on each other.

Teaching at Douglass didn't mean I gave up performing myself. I played with the Redskins Band for 16 wonderful years. During my first year as a teacher, I got a call from Al Winfield, who said his combo was playing at the Cotton Club on Kenilworth Avenue and he needed a drummer immediately. It turned out that his drummer had a big ego and had quit. I hit it off with the other musicians and played with the Altones until Al's death 30 years later. Then the four-piece instrumental group with female vocalist became known as "Roy Battle and the

Altones." They are a wonderful group of people, and I have always considered myself fortunate to have been associated with them.

PART II

MILITARY SERVICE

Man to "Boy" and Back Again

I'd never been far from home or without the support of family and friends until I got my induction notice in the summer of 1943. Then suddenly I found myself alone, choking on the soot of a train bound for the unknown. For the first time in my life, I didn't have a plan, a goal. I had no idea what lay before me. Nothing in my previous life fully prepared me for the challenges I'd have to meet, the bonds I'd ultimately form, or the type of man I'd eventually become.

It often seemed that being in the Army, even after I was accepted for the Tuskegee Institute, was nothing but challenges, many having nothing to do with actually being a soldier. There were ticks and sand and mud and leaky tents to be dealt with. There was also the way the Army gave liberty passes, only to take them back again, which was always frustrating. All of these had to be dealt with while meeting the challenges of actual Army training, which included forced marches with 50-pound packs, learning to fire a weapon, and more importantly, learning to keep my head and rear down while others were firing weapons. The thing that helped me get through was that I finally had a goal: to become a United States Air Force bombardier. That was the biggest challenge of all. I had to learn everything there was to know about the missiles I would be firing, as well as about finding and hitting my target. It was grueling work that required long hours of making calculations before taking off in an old, beat-up plane to practice. In the end it was all worth it. The biggest, most important day of my young life finally rolled around—November 4, 1944—when the silver bombardier wings were pinned on my chest.

As I stood on the platform with my fellow graduates, I realized I probably wouldn't be there if it weren't for them. The bond we had formed through training had carried us all through. When we first got to Tuskegee, we'd been told, "Anything done must be done for the group." During training, we faced real dangers practicing maneuvers set up to simulate actual war conditions. I came to appreciate how much I had to trust my fellow soldiers and how much they relied on me.

This bond helped us face the biggest and, potentially, the most dangerous challenge—racism. I quickly learned that the rampant racism in the military could not be handled by standing in the door and yelling epithets, which had worked with Mr. Bruggeman in Harlem. It could only be handled by sticking together and taking whatever was thrown at us. As much as we loved music, a fellow cadet and I refused to play for base dances after we were hidden from the dancers' sight by tall trees. When a gate guard purposely delayed a busload of us bound for liberty, and demanded, "who said that?" when one of us complained, we all filed off the bus and faced the machine gun the guard had fetched from his guard house. Neither of those incidents made the newspapers. They were too common place. But our reaction to the unlawful ban from the Freeman Air Force Base Officers club did.

While trying to enter the club, one of our officers inadvertently brushed an assistant Provost Marshall. Our officer was arrested, charged, and eventually convicted by general court-martial. But the 101 + 3 of us stuck together, comrades in arms, bonded by common experience. I was and still am very, very proud of the part I played in our fight against racism and segregation. No matter how the racists viewed me, no matter how many called me "boy," I knew that I was a man ... a Tuskegee Airman.

Midland Army Air Base, Midland, Texas, 1944

On one Thursday morning, a special meeting was called that required the attendance of all bombardier/navigation cadets. The room was the type in which all seats were tiered. Down in the center was the podium, a long table, and a covered mockup of something. All of us cadets filed in holding our note pads and pencils. What caught my attention was the fact that also filing in were the heavy brass.

There were at least 20 full colonels, along with majors and captains too numerous to count. I even saw a one-star (brigadier) general in the group. My squadron leader leaned over to me and whispered that all of the officers had flown in from combat for this special meeting.

With such an auspicious audience, we were in high anticipation of hearing from at least a colonel, if not a general. Much to our surprise, at 10 AM sharp, a short corporal strode to the platform with a pointer in hand. He was really dressed; his trousers and shirt had creases on which one could seemingly cut one's hand. His shoes reflected the morning sun and his face glowed a reddish color, which suggested that he had shaved at least five times. He went directly to the microphone, slowly rotated his head from left to right, then, in a "basso profundo" voice, declared, "Sirs, in all the world there are probably 50 men who know more about this object than I do." He then paused and deliberately rotated his head from left to right again, booming out, "But I don't see a damned one of them here in this room." And with that, he slipped the cover off the mockup with a flourish and said, "Gentlemen, I give you the latest model Norden Bomb Sight." The room exploded with applause.

The United States was years ahead of the Allies in this regard. The Allies had no instrument that could deliver bombs from such unbelievable heights (10,000 to 15,000 feet) with uncanny, pinpoint accuracy. Had this been a typical class situation, it could have been very awkward. However, the corporal met the problem head on and the brass was readily able to accept the corporal as a teacher.

Further Memoirs of a Tuskegee Airman

The complete saga of the Tuskegee Airmen, in order to be fully appreciated, must include the three warplanes identified with each phase of the Tuskegee Airmen's Development: P-40, 1942 (99th Pursuit

Squadron); P-51, 1943 (332nd Fighter Group, Red Tails); B-25, 1943 (477th Medium Bombardment Group).

It was my honor to receive my wings and bars as a second lieutenant, upon graduation as a bombardier/navigator, at Midland Air Force Base on November 4, 1944. I was assigned to Squadron 606 at Godman Field, Louisville, Kentucky. (The term "natural high" had a new meaning for me. When I received my wings and bars, I was like a cloud floating on air.)

To be perfectly frank, making history as one of the first Blacks to fly never entered my mind, and fear never gave me pause for thought; I just wanted to keep up with the group and do my duty to my country. I still smile today when I think of my reaction to the first enlisted man who saluted me; I almost put my eye out returning his salute.

My most severe encounter with racism occurred April 5, 1945, when our group was moved to Freeman Field in Seymour, Indiana. We were to receive intense combat and over-the-water training there, prior to being shipped to the Pacific Theater of War. The conflict in Europe was winding down.

The colonel at Freeman Field, upon learning that an all-Black (basically) Air Group was assigned to him, immediately shut down the officers' club in defiance to Army Regulation 210-10, paragraph 19, 1940. He assigned armed guards to all entrances. What was termed "The Freeman Field Mutiny" then occurred. That evening 19 of us attempted to enter the club and were promptly arrested (I'm proud to say that I was in that group). A total of 104 Black officers were placed under barracks arrest and three officers were held to be court-martialed (for having brushed against an arresting officer).

There were threats of trying us for disobeying a direct order in the time of war (ignoring the fact that it was an unlawful order), and promises that we would be hung. Through all of this, I became a man amongst men as we bonded together.

Lieutenant Bill Terry was the only officer found guilty, for jostling a superior officer, at the court-martial. He was sentenced to forfeit 50 dollars a month for three months and was found not guilty for disobeying an order. The rest of us were issued Letters of Reprimand (L.O.R.), which remained in our 201 files until August 1995, when the Honorary Rodney A. Coleman (Assistant Secretary of the Air Force and himself a Tuskegee Airman) announced the Air Force's decision to overturn the court-martial and to expunge the L.O.R.s.

Tuskegee Cleanliness, December 1944

This incident involves a cadet who shall be nameless, for obvious reasons. For the life of me, I couldn't see how Cadet X made it as far as the bombardier/navigator training level with his negligent bathing habits. In classroom theory work, there was always a scramble by us to get to the "window" seats. (The barracks and classrooms were not air-conditioned so the fans were always going full blast.) But, one by one, the other cadets became aware of the offensive odor emitted by Cadet X.

Giving hints about his odor to Cadet X did not seem to work. Notes were left on his bed, instructors alluded to "cleanliness being next to godliness." Finally, a meeting was held by several cadets in the barracks latrine. It was agreed that action would be taken that same night.

After taps sounded, five of the "huskiest" cadets surrounded Cadet X's cot and, at an agreed-upon signal, four of the five cadets flew into action. One each grabbed an arm, while the other two grabbed a leg. The fifth cadet carried the cleaning equipment. When they arrived at the showers, the whole barracks was awakened by the shouting, followed by a roar of approval. All of the shower heads were turned on. All of the cadets were in the buff. They stripped Cadet X of his "skivvies" and proceeded to lather him with a very strong brown soap called "Fels-Naptha." Then a cadet started scrubbing Cadet X with a hard, straw scrub brush. He did not miss a spot. This routine continued for at least

10 minutes. Finally, after a hot rinse, they dropped Cadet X and went to their respective cots, dried themselves, and turned in.

I am very pleased to announce that from that moment on, the "air" around Cadet X was quite healthy. The incident was not reported to the company commander who, incidentally, must have felt good that his words had been so religiously heeded by Cadet X: "Cleanliness is next to godliness."

Godman Field— Air-to-Ground Firing, January 1945

After I had received my wings and commission as a second lieutenant, I was assigned to the B-25J Billy Mitchell Bomber. There were six men in our crew and we were scheduled to fly together on a regular basis. On this particular morning, we were scheduled for "air-to-ground" machine gun firing. My position as bombardier/navigator was in the nose of the airplane. My duties, along with navigating our plane to destination and return, were to drop bombs, singular or salvo (group), safely and correctly. Also I had to defend our plane from frontal attacks with a .50 calibre machine gun in the nose, which I was to man in time of combat. There is quite a lot of responsibility attached to placing one's self behind a .50 calibre machine gun and pulling the trigger. First of all, we machine gunners had to draw on the very intense training that we went through in the "gunnery" phase of our cadet training.

At Tyndall Field, Florida, where we received our gunnery training, there were corporals and sergeants ever ready to assist and teach us. Up there in the bomber, you were by yourself. If you had a mission to destroy a tank unit supported by several platoons of enemy soldiers, you had to interdict and destroy. As the lead gunner, I had to lay down an accurate line of fire, thus enabling the planes following me to zero in and destroy effectively. If my gun jammed, I could not call on a corporal or sergeant to repair the damage. I had to solve those problems myself. Gun jams are sometimes caused by careless loading of shells in the feeder belt. I had to see personally that each round was firmly inserted in the webbing. I had to see that the ammo belt was smoothly loaded in the ammo can, one layer in ribbon fashion on the other. Think of the smooth pattern of cake as the dough is poured into the baking pan.

On this particular morning, we were to wipe out a dug-in enemy platoon, which had occupied a large tract of hilly, underbrush terrain. Our group leader said we could employ a "low level" bombing approach. Then, after releasing our bombs, we would do an 180-degree turn, using our machine guns to wipe out the "hornets nest," our name given to entrenched enemy fire positions. The bombs were to knock out the tanks, trucks, etc. The real danger of this mission was the very low level and shallow angle we had to fly and maintain in order to complete the job. The mountains were a real problem, what with the updrafts and uneven heights, not to mention how many times we had to do an 180-degree turn to try to carry out our orders.

A low-flying aircraft is "meat on the table" to ground troops. They form in squares about 30 to a platoon, aim in the space in front of the plane, and hopefully (for them) you will fly right into the volley. As lead navigator/bombardier and machine gunner, it was my duty to scout the problem and read by air, map out targets of opportunity for the squadron, assign spacing/heights for our planes so that we would-n't shoot each other down, and lastly, decide on the angle of the attack. I figured 500 feet would be low enough because the terrain was very mountainous. I then saw a long break in our path and signaled the for-mation to follow me down to about 300 feet. I figured this low-level approach would permit the bombs to have a "skipping" effect and per-haps hit lower on the target base.

The mission was a success; my squadron completely eliminated the pocket of resistance, destroying enemy tanks, communication facilities, and troops. (As this was a training mission, all targets and soldiers were made of wood). The following morning, we had a pre-flight meeting. The plan was to knock out enemy tanks and troops that were on the move toward our lines. As the pre-flight briefing broke up and we headed for our planes, our line chief came over to me, holding a peculiar piece of metal in his hand. He said, "Lieutenant Battle, this is a little gadget I made for you. I suggest you sit on this. I call it the family jewels saver. First, you set this down." The object was 16 inches long, 20 inches wide, and one inch thick. It looked rather dense and heavy; however it was surprisingly light. "Then you sit on your parachute on top of this," he continued.

"What's it for?" I shouted above the din of the engines. He looked at me, gave me a fiendish smile, saluted, and went towards the hangar.

Checking my chronometer, I noted it was time to "saddle up," so I waved to the other leaders on the flight line, lifted myself through the bottom hatch, secured same, and signaled for the pilots to start to the take-off position. After we were airborne, I crawled up to the nose, took out the sectional map, made several notations, and told the pilot to take a particular heading after the squadron was formed.

We approached the target area at about 2000 feet. I could see the primary targets. We then turned to our initial point (I.P.) and dropped down to the deck to begin our bomb run.

Two planes were making the first run as planned. We dropped to an angle of 30 degrees and started our run. I could see flashes from the rifles of enemy fire. (They were firing blanks, but the smoke gave the scene an unsettling feeling of combat.)

After the bomb runs (I could see that several of the targets, including a really outdated locomotive with freight cars, had been damaged or eliminated), we reformed to begin our strafing attack. I felt pretty good because the fire I was laying down seemed to have found its mark. It was when we pulled up and started to turn to vacate the target area that I heard this "ping, ping, plunk, plunk" noise. It was a metallic sound coming from the bottom of the plane. My crew chief leaned over and yelled in my ear, "Those sounds you hear, Lieutenant, are the ricochet rounds hitting our plane. They are live and very dangerous."

I made a mental note to look up the line chief as soon as post-briefing was over and to express my undying thanks to him for my "family jewels saver," over a dinner at my expense.

Italian Prisoners of War (P.O.W.s)

As I explained in my first book, *Easier Said*, 104 of us officers were placed under arrest at Freeman Field in Seymour, Indiana, for disobeying a direct (but unlawful) order not to go into the base officers' club. This incident is often referred to as "the Mutiny at Freeman Field." The entire event is very well documented in Lieutenant Colonel James C. Warren's treatise, *The Freeman Field Mutiny*.

Aside from the fact that we were humiliated and denied our natural rights to access the base officers' club (as set forth in Army regulations 210-10, paragraph 19, dated 1940, which opened the officers' club on all posts, bases, and stations to all officers), we were placed behind barbed wire with armed guards patrolling the perimeter. However, the most weird and befuddling sight for us was of the Italian prisoners—who had P.O.W. painted on the backs of their dungarees—walking around, smoking, using the post exchange (P.X.), and eating in the regular mess hall, while we bonafide officers were locked up. Rather than needlessly repeat the outcome of the above mess, I'll refer the reader to my first book, *Easier Said*.

Present Involvement with the Tuskegee Airmen, Inc.

I am an active member of the East Coast Chapter of the Tuskegee Airmen, Inc., and have a very intricate role in the Tuskegee Airmen's

Speakers Bureau. My present responsibilities entail, among others, going around to area elementary, middle, and high schools to lecture on positive attitudes. I deal with honesty and character development in spite of handicaps, using my book, *Easier Said*, as a focal point for my presentations. I have also presented these speeches to churches and service organizations, namely the Sea Scouts, the Ruritan Club, the Kiwanis club, the Knights of the Round Table, Friends of the Library, and the United Stated Air Force Museum at Wright-Patterson Air Force Base in Dayton, Ohio.

During the course of the lectures, videos on the "Tuskegee Experience" may also be shown, depicting and explaining the vital parts played by all three elements of the Tuskegee Airmen: the 99th Pursuit Squadron, the 332nd Fighter Group (the Redtails), and the 477th Medium Bomb Group. Their dual roles were fighting overseas in the European Theater of War and the valiant fight on the home front to eradicate segregation in the armed forces.

I am extremely grateful to the following members of the East Coast Chapter of the Tuskegee Airmen, Inc., for taking me personally under their collective wings to guide, counsel, and mentor me in carrying out my responsibilities and obligations related to spreading the exciting, factual history of the Tuskegee Airmen:

Mrs. Cora "Tess" Spooner, Past President
Colonel George "Hank" Henry, United States Air Force, Retired
Major Hank Sanford, United States Air Force, Retired
Major Sergeant Sam Bass, United States Air Force, Retired
Lieutenant Colonel Ivan Ware, United States Air Force, Retired
Lieutenant William "Bill" Broadwater, United States Air Force,
*   Retired*
First Lieutenant Ira O'Neal, United States Air Force, Retired
Colonel Elmer Jones, United States Air Force, Retired

Lieutenant Colonel Woody Crockett, United States Air Force, Retired

Major Bill Wilson, United States Air Force, Retired

Mr. Sam Rhodes

Mr. Cicero Satterfield

Mr. Jim Pryde

Mr. Hamp Johnson

Colonel Taro K. Jones

Lieutenant Colonel Oliver C. Carter

Lieutenant Colonel Leo Gray

Mr. Preston Davis, Senior

Chief Master Sergeant Clarence Turner

Harry (pictured left) and LeRoy
(age eight, pictured right),
Brooklyn, New York, 1928.

LeRoy's Aunt Bert, Uncle Fred,
and mother Margie at
Rockaway Beach,
New York, 1929.

Wedding of Vashti Holt in the spring of 1953. Pictured left to right –
Dorothea Holt, Carol Chaney Holt, Catherine Sollers, Vashti Holt
(bride), James Harrison Holt (father of the bride), Alice Holt
(LeRoy's future wife), Jean Queen, Novene Holt, Karen Moore
(flower girl), and Walter Moore, Jr. (ring bearer).

LeRoy, Jr., and Lisa in concert at Bayridge Inn,
Annapolis, Maryland, May 1972.

Roy's wedding 1995: LeRoy, Jr. (left) and brother Terry (right).

Aunt Bert's 50th birthday in Brooklyn; a very special lady,
she helped to raise LeRoy!

LeRoy and his daughter Dr. Lisa Battle Singletary,
wedding, May 20, 2000.

LeRoy's daughter, Dr. Lisa P. Battle, circa 2006.

Dr. Mary Brown and Thomas Scott marriage,
St. Thomas, Virgin Islands, September 9, 2006.

LeRoy with his grandson Justice, granddaughter Sydney,
and daughter-in-law Kim.

LeRoy and his grandson Justice.

Celebration of Margie Battle Smith's 100th birthday:
(left to right) Karen Matthews, Alice Battle, Bea Polin.

Master Sergeant Greg Binford and his wife Eileen at the celebration
of Margie Smith's 100th birthday.

LeRoy's mother Margie Battle Smith, 102-years-old, talking to two of her great grandchildren, Leroy III and Sydney. Also shown are Sheryl Luttrell and Phillip Wood.

LeRoy's mother Margie reacts to her introduction to the crowd. Otis Winfield and Sheryl Luttrell are in the background.

LeRoy with his mother Margie, 102-years-old.

LeRoy's mother, Margie Battle Smith, who was born on May 12, 1903, and passed away at the age of 103 on November 11, 2006.

First Lieutenant Claude Davis,
Tuskegee Bomber Pilot,
477 Bomb Group, who now
resides in Inglewood, California,
and holds a high position as a
senior broker in real estate.

Cadet Battle, 1944.

Singer, dancer, and actress Lena Horne at Tuskegee, 1944.

Bombardier navigation school walking tour, 1944, Midland, Texas. LeRoy (right) and Benny from Ohio (left). For any rule infraction, such as reporting late to class, cadets had to walk up and down the parade grounds for 50 minutes and rest 10 minutes.

Graduation day from Tyndall Army Air Corps Base, Panama City, Florida, July 25, 1944. LeRoy was certified as an air gunner. His next move was to Midland Army Air Force base in Midland, Texas, for bombardier/navigation wings and a commission as a second lieutenant in the Army Air Corps.

Graduation day from gunnery school at Tyndall Field, Florida, in 1944. Pictured from left to right are Jarrett, Farrell, and LeRoy.

Godman Field, Kentucky, under arrest for mutiny, April 1945: LeRoy is in the center at the top of the stairs.

CADET LACKLAND 1955

PHU CAT RVN 1970

BLIND BAT THAILAND 1966

HQ PACAF 1977

The honors trail of Colonel George "Hank" Henry, Tuskegee Airman.

2ND LT. LeROY A. BATTLE
PREPARING FOR FLIGHT
TUSKEGEE...MOTEN FIELD
AUG. 20, 1945...CLASS 46B

Second Lieutenant LeRoy A. Battle preparing for flight, Tuskegee
Moten Field, August 20, 1945.

United States of America

Certification of

Military Service

This certifies that	Leroy A. Battle 42 032 752
was a member of the	Army of the United States
from	August 25, 1943
to	November 3, 1944
Service was terminated by	Honorable Discharge
Last Grade, Rank, or Rating	Aviation Cadet
Active Service Dates	Same as Above

Given at St. Louis, Missouri, on October 30, 1972

National Personnel Records Center
(Military Personnel Records)
National Archives and Records Service
General Services Administration

THE ADMINISTRATOR OF GENERAL SERVICES ADMINISTRATION IS THE CUSTODIAN OF THIS PERSON'S MILITARY RECORD.
(This form not valid without official seal.)

GSA FORM 6954

LeRoy's honorable discharge from the military.

LeRoy at Morgan State College, 1948. He is shown in the drum section
at the right bottom of the photo, standing up and wearing sunglasses.

LeRoy's graduation photo, Morgan State College, June 1950.

Carl Hawkins, former Douglass Band member: "Thank you, Mr. Battle. I survived the Korean War by playing in the band!"

Douglass Elementary Junior Senior High School Majorettes, 1950: (far left) Alice Harper, (next) Wilma Humbles, (front) unknown, (next right) Anne Tolson; (back row, left) unknown, (middle) Vivian Proctor, (right) Susie Smith.

Senior band ensemble, Frederick Douglass Elementary Junior Senior High School, 1953.

Wilma Humbles, drum majorette, Frederick Douglass Elementary Junior Senior High School, 1953.

Douglass Eagle Band ready to strut in Takoma Park Parade, 1955:
Drum Major Barbara Parker and other twirlers—
(left to right) Susie Proctor, Frances Jackson, and Catherine Mason.

Tympanist Joan Bell, 1956.

Douglass Eagle Band preparing to step off in Capitol Classic Parade
Washington, DC, 1956.

Barbara Adams, lead majorette twirler for the Douglass Eagle
marching band, is shown receiving a first place trophy from radio
personality "Pick" Temple, Naval Powder Factory, Indian Head,
Maryland, October 13, 1957.

Douglass Eagles "B" Band, 1960.

First chair clarinets of Douglass Concert Band, Gloria Pinkney (left)
and Tondaleya Proctor (right).

Douglass Eagles show off their new drums circa 1963.
LeRoy is pictured on the far right.

Joseph Ennis, co-worker of
LeRoy's and organizer of the
Frederick Douglass drill team.

William "Bill" Reid,
Bandmaster, Wiley H. Bates
High School, Annapolis,
Maryland.

THE BALTIMORE AFRO-AMERICAN, APRIL 2, 1963

DUE AT COPPIN — The Douglass High School Concert Band of Upper Marlboro, Md., will be presented in a concert at Coppin State Teachers College on Thursday, April 4, at 11 a.m. The concert is part of an exchange series between the two schools.

The Douglass High School Concert Band plays at Coppin State Teachers College, April 1963.

Douglass concert band circa 1963.

Christmas parade, Silver Springs, Maryland 1964.
The Douglas Eagle Band won first place.

Rosa Wills with future majorette, 1964.

The Worst Experience
I've Ever Had With A Bumble Bee

By GLENDORA DAVIS

Percussionist, "Eagle" Band
Frederick Douglass Jr.-Sr. H.S.
Upper Marlboro, Maryland

1964

Teacher and friends, I know you all know
Of a gay little song that fits springtime so.
The name is the "Bumble Bee," a devilish thing,
That when played at 1:50, makes a marimba ring.

For almost two months of this school year,
I fought with that bumble bee, without any fear;
Worked it out slowly, and up to tempo —
The more that I practiced, the faster I'd go.

With my able accompanist doing his part,
When we played it together, 'twas musical art.
We got it expertly, and what do you know?
At the March County Festival, we two took the show.

Then came that great time, of the school P.T.A.,
When the yearly band concert highlighted the day.
The next on the program? My marimba solo —
I should have been joyful, but I felt oh, so low!

But I wasn't nervous, for reasons unknown,
Forgetting the audience, I trod clouds alone.
Then Rodney said, "Next is an instrumental song
That needs no introduction, please don't hum along."

"A beautiful introduction," to myself I said,
"Live up to it now, Douglass percussion forges ahead!"
So then we got started; and oh, my soul!!
I let go of notes I was supposed to hold.

Since that bad start was an over-sized flop,
We signaled each other — "We'd better stop."
We started again, a futile try.
He left me behind, and I gave him an eye.

I looked at him, and he looked at me;
For our notes were as divided as a musical sea.

I prayed for a hole to come in the floor,
Because Heaven knows, I *knew that score.*

I wanted to run, but I knew if I did
I would just be acting like an under-aged kid.
"A professional air," Mr. Battle would say,
"Fools most people, so — play, play, play."

As those guiding words ran through my mind,
I captured the nerve I'd been trying to find.
The blame was on both — the accompanist and me,
And I heard someone say, "Please swat that bee."

That great big audience looked just like a mob,
Freezing my tears to a choked-off sob.
I said to myself, "It can't get you down;
You'll get IT, and how, when you try this last round."

So we went it again, for a last — third time.
This was as smooth as a nursery rhyme.
As that "Bumble Bee" went from first flower to last,
It was making good time, and making it fast.

Then it came to an end, and with thunderous applause;
I bowed and I smiled, with no hint of a pause.
I wanted to die, but I couldn't let them know,
For I still had the rest of the concert to go.

We had had our fight, that bumble bee and I,
Next time, I'll make it a "Butterfly."
For it will be more gentle, but better still,
A nice fat turtle, on a long steep hill.

For it'll be much slower, as you can be sure.
And it will be something, the accompanist can endure.
Now you all know what a "Bumble Bee" can do,
So, I'll just leave — the rest to you!

"MUSIC LESSONS"

By Charles Werner
George Peabody College
Nashville, Tennessee

While studying about children's literature recently, I was reminded of my own two daughters and how typical they are when it comes to practicing their music. A little poem came to mind, and I sat down and penned it as follows:

Do you have to take piano lessons
like me?
If you do, then I'm sure you'll agree
That practicing those old lessons
every day
Surely does use up all my time to
play.

Every day when I'm playing outside
And Mother. calls to me,
I run and find a place to hide;
'Cause I know what she wants, you
see.

"It's time to practice!" I hear her
say.

But by that time, I'm far away.
"Oh," I say to myself, "what's the
use!"
I may as well face the music!" and
call a truce.

"There is no right way to do a
wrong thing." —Seneca

"The Worst Experience I've Ever Had with a Bumble Bee"
by Glenora Davis, percussionist, Eagle Band, Frederick Douglass
Elementary Junior Senior High School, Upper Marlboro, Maryland—
published in *School Musician*, a nationwide education magazine.

Our High Flying Eagles Prance a Bit Too . . .

JOAN JOHNSON
Twirler

DARLENE CORNISH
Twirler

JOYCE FRIEND
"Golden Eagle Girl"

SHELLY COTTMAN
Twirler

RUTH MOLOCK
Twirler

Douglass Eagles twirlers: Joan Johnson and Darleen Cornish (top),
Shelly Cottman and Ruth Molock (bottom), Joyce Friend (far right).

Practice for the 1965 World's Fair.

Douglass Eagle Band dress rehearsal for trip
to 1965 World's Fair in New York.

The Douglass Eagle Band won first place at the 1965 World's Fair in
New York. Both bandleaders, Silverene Johnson (left) and Carl
Winsor (right), are the "cream of the crop."

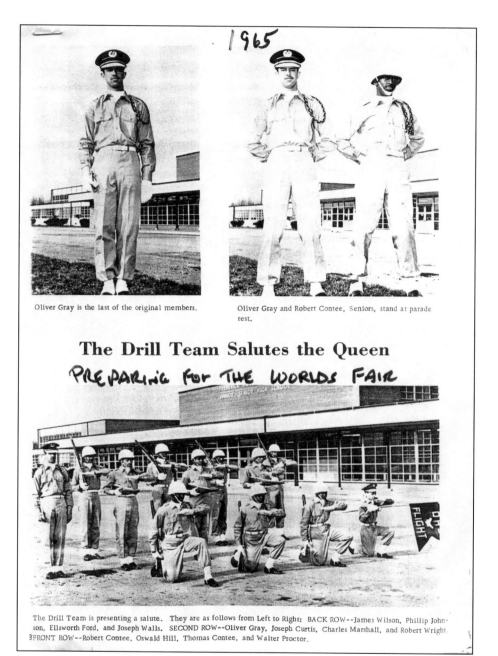

Oliver Gray is the last of the original members.

Oliver Gray and Robert Contee, Seniors, stand at parade rest.

The Drill Team Salutes the Queen

PREPARING FOR THE WORLDS FAIR

The Drill Team is presenting a salute. They are as follows from Left to Right: BACK ROW--James Wilson, Phillip Johnson, Ellsworth Ford, and Joseph Walls. SECOND ROW--Oliver Gray, Joseph Curtis, Charles Marshall, and Robert Wright. FRONT ROW--Robert Contee, Oswald Hill, Thomas Contee, and Walter Proctor.

Frederick Douglass Drill Team circa 1965: (top left) Oliver Gray; (top right) Oliver Gray and Robert Contee; (bottom, left to right, back row) James Wilson, Phillip Johnson, Ellsworth Ford, and Joseph Walls; (second row) Oliver Gray, Joseph Curtis, Charles Marshall, and Robert Wright; (front row) Robert Contee, Oswald Hill, Thomas Contee, and Walter Proctor.

First Chair musicians, Douglass Eagle Band, 1965.

Former majorette Phyllis Ervin, now supervisor of social studies for the Prince George's County public schools, circa 1997.

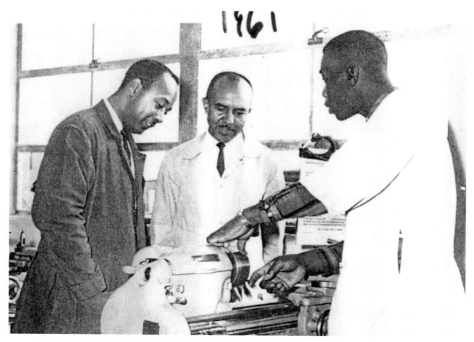

(left to right) Jack is a former Douglass Bandsman (tenor sax);
Clio Whitley was LeRoy's former mentor;
William Blount was a very close friend of LeRoy's.

Al Winfield, founder of the Altones, gigging at the Maryland Inn,
Annapolis, Maryland. LeRoy is on the drums in the background.

The Altones at a gig at Howard University, Washington, DC, 1964:
(left to right) Malvin, piano; Billy, bass; Al, alto sax;
LeRoy Battle, drums; Ike, tenor sax; Maurice, trumpet.

Al "Hot Poppa" Carter, Altones
combo, 1980.

Marilyn Carlson, vocalist for
LeRoy Battle and The Altones,
1980.

LeRoy Battle and the Altones, 1980: (left to right)
Paul Case, keyboards; Dennis Davis, tenor sax; Marilyn Carlson,
vocalist; Jack King, bassist; LeRoy Battle, drums.

Artie Dicks, vocalist with Roy Battle and The Altones, 1985.
Artie was a former Ink Spots singer, the famous quartet that made
"If I Didn't Care" famous.

The Altones perform at Truxton Park for Seniors Picnic, 1990:
(left to right) LeRoy Battle, drums; Paul Case, keyboards;
Artie Dicks, vocalist; Jack King, bassist; Dennis Davis, tenor sax.

The Altones concert in the park at Havre de Grace, Maryland,
July 2005: (left to right) Dennis Davis, Marilyn Carlson, LeRoy
Battle, Jack King, and Blake Cramer from the Navy Academy.

Photographer Leo P. Heppner and LeRoy circa 1999.

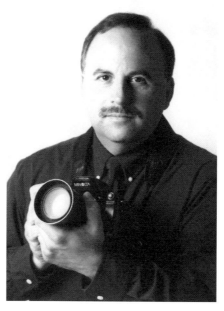

Leo P. Heppner, official
photographer for LeRoy Battle
and the Altones.

LeRoy receiving the Counselor of the Year award, 1977,
from George Robinson, Superintendent of Schools,
Prince George's County, Maryland.

LeRoy in the *Sunday Capital* newspaper, 1996.

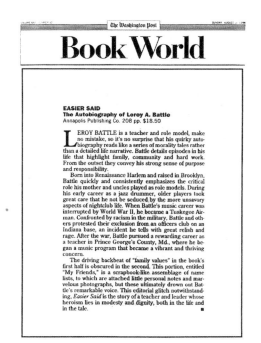

Book review from *The Washington Post*, August 1996.

Commendation from the Board of County Commissioners,
St. Mary's County, Maryland.

BALTIMORE COUNTY PUBLIC SCHOOLS

Anthony G. Marchione, Superintendent   6901 Charles Street   Towson, Maryland 21204-3711

May 2, 1996

Mr. LeRoy A. Battle
4689 Sands Road
Harwood, MD 20776

Dear Mr. Battle:

    I apologize for not responding to your letter sooner. I did appreciate receiving a copy of your autobiography entitled, <u>Easier Said</u>. I read it several weeks ago but have not had the opportunity to respond to you. I plan to share this copy of your autobiography with our Assistant Superintendent for Curriculum and Instruction. I agree with you that it would be a book that we would want to encourage our middle and high school students to read. When we have had the book reviewed I will ask Dr. Bavaria to let you know how we might use this book in our program of studies.

    Thank you for taking the time to write to us. Best wishes.

Sincerely,

Anthony G. Marchione
Superintendent

AGM:ebi
c: Dr. Richard Bavaria

Letter from Superintendent Anthony G. Marchione, Baltimore County Public Schools.

Prince George's County Council of Social Studies Award Banquet:
LeRoy A. Battle, author of *Easier Said*, and
Dr. Charles Christian, author of *Black Saga*, 1997.

East Coast Chapter of the Tuskegee Airmen, Cora "Tess" Spooner,
President, 1998: dedicating "Charles Herbert Flowers," a new school
in that Tuskegee Airman's name. LeRoy is at far right.

(left to right) Janie Moore Gholston, LeRoy, Elinor Ford,
former teachers at Douglass High School who taught with LeRoy
in the 1950s and 1960s.

(left to right) Janie Moore, LeRoy, Margeurite Simpson,
former teachers who taught with LeRoy.

Douglass High School honors LeRoy, September 2000:
Band Director Alphonso Giles is seated to the right of LeRoy.

Tuskegee Airmen (LeRoy, top right) visit F.B.I. Headquarters,
September 29, 2000.

Tuskegee Airmen at F.B.I. Headquarters, September 29, 2000:
(left to right) S. Rhodes, L. Gray, LeRoy, Valentine, Hank.

Marilyn Cooper and Vashti Holt (LeRoy's sister-in-law) preparing
food at the Battle's home for the Tuskegee Airmen's picnic honoring
Colonel Leo Gray, September 2000.

Visit to F.B.I. Headquarters, September 29, 2000:
(front row, left to right) Section Chief Dennis Weaver, LeRoy Battle,
Sam Rhodes, Leo Gray, J. T. Valentine, George "Hank" Henry.

General R. A. Huck expressing his profound thanks to LeRoy for
speaking to his entire command.

Sergeant Ryad Naseer, host assigned to LeRoy at the event.

Ms. Theresa Fitzpatrick, Director, Community Relations United
States Southern Command, and LeRoy.

Master Sergeant Garrett Edmonds, Assistant Executive Officer to
Chief of Staff; LeRoy; Lieutenant Colonel Stanley Brown.

(front, left to right) Sergeant Pagan; LeRoy; Nivia Butler,
Deputy Chief of Protocol ; (back) Sergeant Williams.

General R. A. Hucks, Chief of Staff, Southern Command (Marines); LeRoy; Robert Matthews (LeRoy's best friend, who accompanied LeRoy to Miami, Florida, for his speaking engagement).

Tuskegee Airman LeRoy Beeler and his wife Odessa—New Years 2005.

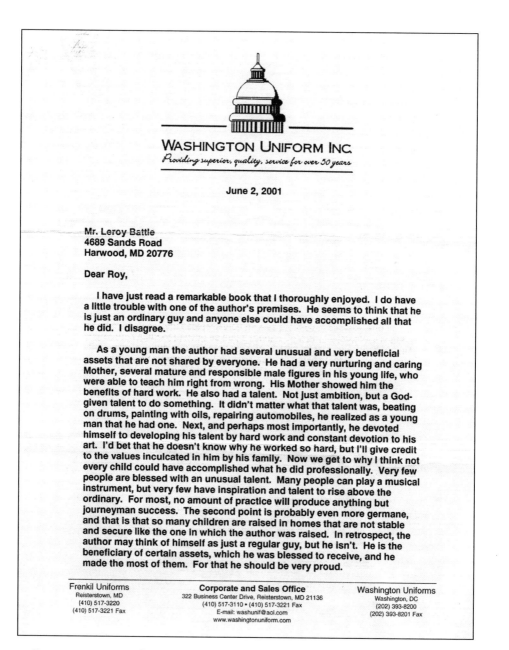

WASHINGTON UNIFORM INC.
Providing superior, quality, service for over 50 years

June 2, 2001

Mr. Leroy Battle
4689 Sands Road
Harwood, MD 20776

Dear Roy,

I have just read a remarkable book that I thoroughly enjoyed. I do have a little trouble with one of the author's premises. He seems to think that he is just an ordinary guy and anyone else could have accomplished all that he did. I disagree.

As a young man the author had several unusual and very beneficial assets that are not shared by everyone. He had a very nurturing and caring Mother, several mature and responsible male figures in his young life, who were able to teach him right from wrong. His Mother showed him the benefits of hard work. He also had a talent. Not just ambition, but a God-given talent to do something. It didn't matter what that talent was, beating on drums, painting with oils, repairing automobiles, he realized as a young man that he had one. Next, and perhaps most importantly, he devoted himself to developing his talent by hard work and constant devotion to his art. I'd bet that he doesn't know why he worked so hard, but I'll give credit to the values inculcated in him by his family. Now we get to why I think not every child could have accomplished what he did professionally. Very few people are blessed with an unusual talent. Many people can play a musical instrument, but very few have inspiration and talent to rise above the ordinary. For most, no amount of practice will produce anything but journeyman success. The second point is probably even more germane, and that is that so many children are raised in homes that are not stable and secure like the one in which the author was raised. In retrospect, the author may think of himself as just a regular guy, but he isn't. He is the beneficiary of certain assets, which he was blessed to receive, and he made the most of them. For that he should be very proud.

Frenkil Uniforms   **Corporate and Sales Office**   Washington Uniforms
Reisterstown, MD   322 Business Center Drive, Reisterstown, MD 21136   Washington, DC
(410) 517-3220   (410) 517-3110 • (410) 517-3221 Fax   (202) 393-8200
(410) 517-3221 Fax   E-mail: washunif@aol.com   (202) 393-8201 Fax
                                     www.washingtonuniform.com

Letter to LeRoy from Phillip Simpkin, Washington Uniform, Inc.
(continued on next page)

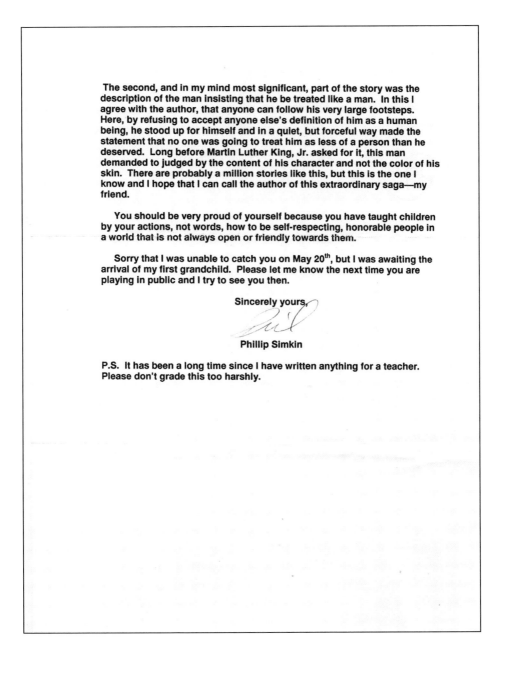

The second, and in my mind most significant, part of the story was the description of the man insisting that he be treated like a man. In this I agree with the author, that anyone can follow his very large footsteps. Here, by refusing to accept anyone else's definition of him as a human being, he stood up for himself and in a quiet, but forceful way made the statement that no one was going to treat him as less of a person than he deserved. Long before Martin Luther King, Jr. asked for it, this man demanded to judged by the content of his character and not the color of his skin. There are probably a million stories like this, but this is the one I know and I hope that I can call the author of this extraordinary saga—my friend.

You should be very proud of yourself because you have taught children by your actions, not words, how to be self-respecting, honorable people in a world that is not always open or friendly towards them.

Sorry that I was unable to catch you on May 20th, but I was awaiting the arrival of my first grandchild. Please let me know the next time you are playing in public and I try to see you then.

Sincerely yours,

Phillip Simkin

P.S. It has been a long time since I have written anything for a teacher. Please don't grade this too harshly.

C.A. Dutch Ruppersberger
2nd District, Maryland
Member of Congress
March 10, 2005

Mr. Leroy A. Battle
4689 Sands Road
Harwood, Maryland 20776

Dear Mr. Battle:

On behalf of a grateful nation, I would like to present you with this copy of your tribute in the Congressional Record. This is a token of our appreciation for all you have done for the United States of America.

I am honored to have the opportunity to acknowledge the sacrifices and achievements you have made for this country. I am proud of your service and of your continued dedication to Maryland's communities.

Your hardships will not be forgotten and your legacies will live on with future generations who will remember the Tuskegee Airmen for their bravery and fortitude in a time of war. Thank you for your service in those extraordinary times. Many flew out into that blue void, but you brought them home again. Yours truly was the Greatest Generation.

Sincerely,

C.A. Dutch Ruppersberger
Member of Congress

CADR:dcl

Letter from C.A. Dutch Ruppersberger, Maryland Congressman,
March 10, 2005.

The Congress of the United States

Requests the honor of your presence at a

Congressional Gold Medal Award Ceremony

in honor of

The Tuskegee Airmen

on Thursday, the twenty-ninth day of March

Two thousand seven

One o'clock in the afternoon

The Rotunda

Capitol of the United States

Washington, District of Columbia

Please arrive by 11:30 a.m. South Visitor's Entrance

R.S.V.P. to (202) 226-8488 by Friday, March 16
This Invitation admits the bearer and one guest
Ticket will be issued upon receipt and is non-transferable

Reception to follow in Longworth House Office Building, Room 1100

LeRoy's invitation to the Congressional Gold Medal Award Ceremony from the Congress of the United States. The Congressional Gold Medal is the nation's most distinguished civilian award bestowed by the United States Congress on those individuals who embody the best qualities in America's heritage. Before it can be awarded, legislation must be approved by Congress and signed into law by the President. Congress first awarded the Congressional Gold Medal to George Washington in 1776.

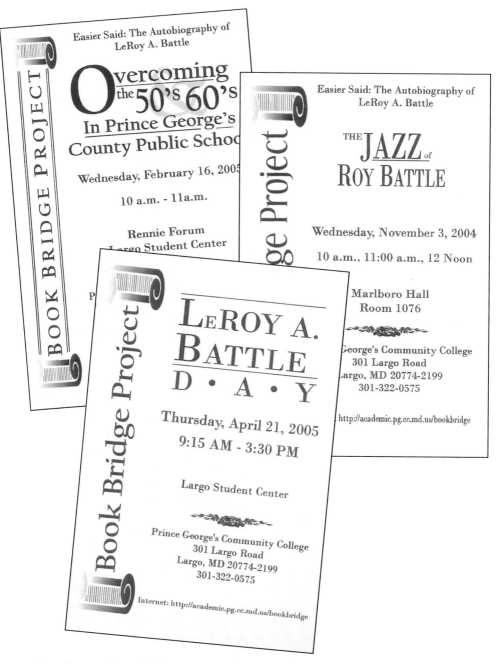

Brochures from LeRoy A. Battle Day, The Jazz of Roy Battle, and "Overcoming the '50s and '60s in Prince George's County Public School," hosted by the Book Bridge Project at Prince George's Community College in Largo, Maryland.

Veterans' Day at Galesville Heritage Museum 2005:
LeRoy, Delegate Virginia Claggett, Jack Smith.

Arleen Dent Winfield speaking at the Salute to LeRoy A. Battle.

Dr. Beatrice Tignor (Douglass Eagle band alumna), Chair, Board of Education, Prince George's County, at LeRoy A. Battle Day, Prince George's Community College, May 2005.

Lawrence, Dick, Gregg, Ned, and Whit play at LeRoy Battle Day, Prince George's County Community College, May 2005.

Dr. Mary P. Brown, host of LeRoy A. Battle Day, Prince George's
County Community College, May 2005.

Elijah Thorne presenting a gift to LeRoy during the celebration of
his life and service to the community.

(left to right) Gilford Tolson, Madeline Woods, Phillip Woods,
Dr. Mary Brown celebrating LeRoy A. Battle Day,
Prince George's County Community College, May 2005.

Frederick Douglass majorettes performing
in honor of LeRoy, May 2005.

Drum major Shariva Smith, senior;
Barry McCullough is shown behind LeRoy.

Ned Judy (keyboard) and Whit Williams (tenor sax) perform
in honor of LeRoy.

Theodora Brown Origone,
former Douglass High School drum majorette.

Master Sergeant Greg Binford and wife Eileen
at LeRoy A. Battle Day.

Salute to LeRoy A. Battle: (left to right) Joseph Ennis, Eloyce Ervin, Phyllis Evans (hidden face), Lina Bowers, Major Charles Bowers.

Former band member Donald G. Tolson, Sr., Dorothea Smith, Reverend William T. Newman.

Reverend William T. Newman at the Salute to LeRoy A. Battle.

Dr. Stephen Hiltabidle, a great surgeon who saved LeRoy's life,
with wife Mary.

Sheryl Luttrell, a loyal family friend.

LeRoy's nephew, Forrest Holt, a great friend indeed.

Donald "Groucho" Gilford Tolson, a former Douglass band member,
who made the Salute to LeRoy A. Battle happen.

Dorothea Smith, a true visionary and champion for students.

Gilford Tolson, Sr., introducing Reverend William T. Newman
at Salute to LeRoy A. Battle, August 27, 2005,
at Waldorf Jaycees Center.

Jane Robinson (left) and Gwen Smith (right), former teachers who
attended the ceremony.

Bob Price, musician; Dora Halton, math teacher;
Joseph Ennis, math teacher and drill team instructor.

Reverend William T. Newman, LeRoy, Dr. Mary Brown.

Remarks
Leroy Battle Celebration

Thank you _____

First, giving honor to God who is the author and finisher of this and all our days; and to Mr. Leroy Battle whose life and legacy we celebrate today; and to family, friends and neighbors assembled here, good afternoon.

One more time my loving husband has given me the opportunity to speak for the two of us to publicly say to you Mr. Battle what a warm spot we have in our hearts for you, and to speak the words of thanks giving for your touch in Tom's life which began with the friendship formed in the marching band at Douglas and continues to now.

For those of you who know us and for those of you we will meet Tom has retired from federal service and now spends very rewarding days at the Body of Christ Farm in Charles County with Father Pittman as the executive Director of Housing while I criss-cross the tri-county area keeping up with buyers and sellers of real estate in this fluid market we are experiencing.

When Mr. Battle came to our community as a young energetic teacher most of us at that time were on a farm and the criss-crossing that was done had to do with the planting and harvesting and keeping the real estate called farm productive. Boots, as many call him, saw musicians in a marching band as he drove into the county pass hot green fields of tobacco being criss-crossed by students from the school where he was going to teach, where no marching band had even been established. Mr. Battle shared with me a story of how he spent summers early in his teaching career visiting families on farms in the county to meet the parents of the students he would recruit to the marching band he formed. One family he visited was that of George and Katie Addison living at the time on 301 near the weigh station. During his visit with my husband's parents he won their respect, trust and support resulting in 6 of their 10 children being excused from farm chores briefly to learn to play a musical instrument and to march in a band.

Today most of us have left the farm to live in subdivisions and planned communities. Anyone wanting to go back to a farm to live see me later and I'll tell you about a 20 acre farm on the market I will be happy to sell you. We aren't living on a farm, we're not playing musical instruments, and we're not marching in any band. These activities from our past however are a part of the fabric that makes us who we are. Just for a moment I want you to see your selves as beautiful quilts. I'm a quilt, you're a quilt, Mr. Battle is a quilt. Everyone in this room is a quilt. Now, focus on the thread in your quilt that represents the farm, and another thread that represents the musical instrument you learned to play or the position you had in the marching band, and another thread for the learning time at Douglas. Very gently and careingly weaving thru your quilt picture a smooth bright colored ribbon (you name the color you want the ribbon to be). That ribbon that has blended in so well represents Mr. Leroy Battle. Each of us as a quilt has him in us because he GAVE OF HIMSELF to help us grow.

Now, I ask you to join me by standing and raising your glasses in a toast to our teacher, friend, and good neighbor who when he came to our community of farmers, saw musicians and Douglas has been marching every since.

Love to you

Dilaren Addison

Wife of

Thomas Addison

Remarks, LeRoy Battle Celebration

LeRoy receives Champion of Courage Award
from the Honorable Kweisi Mfume.

Major General Craig D. Hackett presents LeRoy with the Honorable
Order of Saint Michael, Army Aviation Association of America, 2005.

(left to right) Katie Addison, Alberta Addison, Delores Addison. Katie and Alberta both played clarinet in the Douglass High School Band. Delores' husband, Thomas, played trombone.

Agnes C. Powell, former Douglass High School Band member, now a big-time attorney.

Musician Bob Price with LeRoy.

Dr. Mary L. Brown presenting LeRoy with a gift.

Charles McMillan, former teacher and long-time friend of LeRoy's.

Part of the wonderful crowd at LeRoy's ceremony.

Lawrence Newman, outstanding former bandsman
of Douglass High School.

Delegate James Proctor of Prince George's County. His wife,
Gwendolyn, was a great Douglass High School drum majorette.

Joe Webb, the man with the silver voice.

Elaine Proctor Blackwell—tiny and a teacher of physical education,
but she could handle 80 girls in one session with
no behavior problems.

Gwendolyn Smith, former co-worker at Douglass
and a great teacher!

Lawrence and Linda Newman—Lawrence is a former
Douglass band member.

Joy Branham Pryde, wife of Tuskegee Airman Jim Pryde;
friends always!

Ms. Bernadette Tolson, sharing a moment with LeRoy.

Dr. Beatrice Tignor, Chair, Board
of Education, Prince George's
Sam Bass, Tuskegee Airman.   County, and former Douglass High
band member.

Billy Tolson, former baritone horn player
in LeRoy's Douglass Eagle Band.

Mozella Lawing Harris, science teacher at Frederick Douglass Elementary Junior Senior High School, a true friend of the Douglass Eagle Band circa 1961.

Tuskegee Airman Major Bill Peterson and his wife Gloria.

Barbara Parker Isaacs, the queen of all Douglass high drum majors, the crème de la crème.

Karril Kornheiser (Tony's wife), LeRoy, and Tony Kornheiser. Tony is a television sportscaster and the co-host of "Pardon the Interruption" with Michael Wilbon on ESPN. LeRoy's band played for daughter Elizabeth's Bat Mitzvah.

The original Tuskegee Airmen at the Pentagon November 11, 2005.

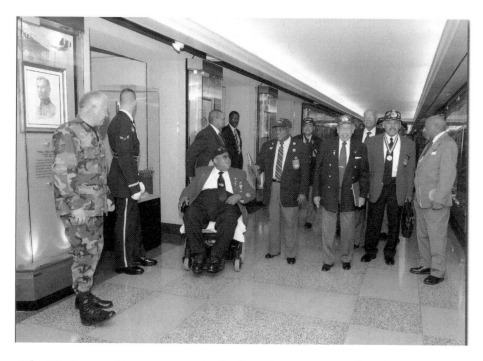

The Tuskegee Airmen were invited to the Pentagon by the Secretary
of Defense on November 11, 2005.

Champions of Courage Breakfast honoring LeRoy A. Battle
(Baltimore, 2005): (left to right) Mayor of Shadyside, Maryland,
Mohan Grover, nephew Forrest Holt, LeRoy A. Battle,
Sheryl Luttrell, and Executive Secretary Elaine Matthews.

Champions of Courage Breakfast honoring LeRoy A. Battle
(Baltimore, 2005): (standing left to right) grandson Justice Battle,
grandson LeRoy A. Battle III, Mayor of Shadyside, Maryland,
Mohan Grover, granddaughter Sydney Battle, and (seated) honoree
Tuskegee Airman LeRoy A. Battle.

To LeRoy Battle
With best wishes,   WHITE 11/11/05
                                                       HOUSE

LeRoy with President Bush at the White House, November 11, 2005.

Tuskegee Airman LeRoy Battle at the Pentagon with Secretary of
State Donald Rumsfield, November 11, 2005.

LeRoy and Sarah Sherman McGrail, June 2006. Sarah is the author of five books, who owns and operates her own publishing house, Cozy Harbor Press, in Southport, Maine. She and LeRoy have been friends since 1996, when they were unexpectedly brought together due to the subject matter of their first books, World War Two.

Sarah's children on vacation in Belize in 2006:
(left to right) Abby, Jake, nephew Hunter, Sherm, and niece Kali.
They started the LeRoy Battle Fan Club—Maine branch.

Compton O. Wright, Dr. Ida Clark, Rosa Green, and Irma Howard at
the Salute to LeRoy A. Battle, August 27, 2006.

Madeline Woods, Bishop Hamilton Edwards, Phillip Woods.

The Senate of Maryland
ANNAPOLIS, MARYLAND 21401

JANET GREENIP
33rd Legislative District
Anne Arundel County

Education, Health, and
Environmental Affairs Committee

April 3, 2007

James Senate Office Building
11 Bladen Street, Room 321
Annapolis, Maryland 21401
410-841-3568 · 301-858-3568
1-800-492-7122 *Ext.* 3568
Fax 410-841-3067

Mr. Leroy Battle
4689 Sands Rd
Hardwood, MD
20776-9428

Dear Mr. Battle:

Please accept my sincere congratulations for receiving the
nation's highest civilian honor, the Congressional Gold Medal,
at the Capital Rotunda in Washington on March 29th.

Your service to the United States during World War II as a
Tuskegee Airman, despite discrimination, is a great inspiration
to us all. I thank you for commitment to serve and for the road
you paved for future opportunities for African Americans.
Finally, as a former educator myself, I admire your career as a
teacher, counselor and administrator in our Maryland schools.

Once again, congratulations and thank you for your service.

Sincerely,

Janet Greenip
Senator, Legislative District 33

JG/bap

Congratulations letter from Janet Greenip, Senator, Legislative
District 33, Annapolis, Maryland, to LeRoy.

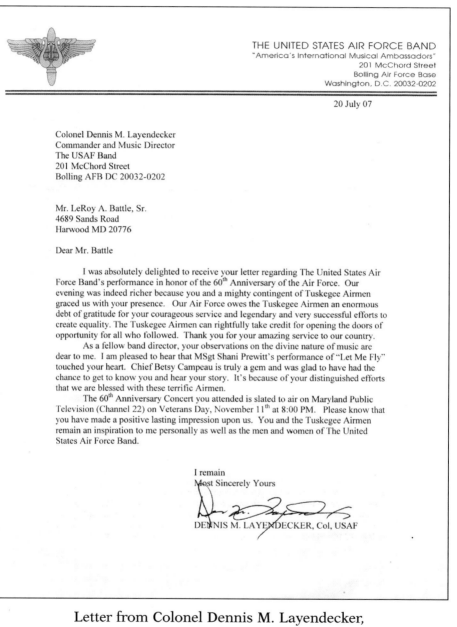

THE UNITED STATES AIR FORCE BAND
"America's International Musical Ambassadors"
201 McChord Street
Bolling Air Force Base
Washington, D.C. 20032-0202

20 July 07

Colonel Dennis M. Layendecker
Commander and Music Director
The USAF Band
201 McChord Street
Bolling AFB DC 20032-0202

Mr. LeRoy A. Battle, Sr.
4689 Sands Road
Harwood MD 20776

Dear Mr. Battle

    I was absolutely delighted to receive your letter regarding The United States Air Force Band's performance in honor of the 60th Anniversary of the Air Force. Our evening was indeed richer because you and a mighty contingent of Tuskegee Airmen graced us with your presence. Our Air Force owes the Tuskegee Airmen an enormous debt of gratitude for your courageous service and legendary and very successful efforts to create equality. The Tuskegee Airmen can rightfully take credit for opening the doors of opportunity for all who followed. Thank you for your amazing service to our country.
    As a fellow band director, your observations on the divine nature of music are dear to me. I am pleased to hear that MSgt Shani Prewitt's performance of "Let Me Fly" touched your heart. Chief Betsy Campeau is truly a gem and was glad to have had the chance to get to know you and hear your story. It's because of your distinguished efforts that we are blessed with these terrific Airmen.
    The 60th Anniversary Concert you attended is slated to air on Maryland Public Television (Channel 22) on Veterans Day, November 11th at 8:00 PM. Please know that you have made a positive lasting impression upon us. You and the Tuskegee Airmen remain an inspiration to me personally as well as the men and women of The United States Air Force Band.

I remain
Most Sincerely Yours

DENNIS M. LAYENDECKER, Col, USAF

**Letter from Colonel Dennis M. Layendecker,
United States Air Force Band, to LeRoy.**

(left to right) Paul Carter, Joy Branham Pryde, LeRoy Battle, James
W. Pryde, Artie McNeil...Tuskegee all.

A new sign for the music wing and a plaque in LeRoy's honor.

LeRoy and the Honorable Marilynn Bland,
Council Member, District 9.

LeRoy with James Proctor, Maryland Delegate.

LeRoy is presented his award by the Honorable Marilynn Bland,
Council Member, District 9.

The audience at the music wing dedication,
Saturday, October 6, 2007.

The Douglass High School chorus,
under the direction of Mrs. Marilyn Walls.

LeRoy and former Douglass bandsman Walter Savoy.

LeRoy takes the microphone and says a few words.

LeRoy and his wife Alice with his dedication plaque.

Former Douglass bandmember Donald Gilford "Groucho" Tolson.

Rudolph Saunders, principal of Frederick Douglass High School,
at the music wing dedication, October 6, 2007.

LeRoy with the Chairman of the Board of Education,
R. Owen Johnson, Jr.

The former Frederick Douglass bandsmen covering years 1950–1965
are pictured with Mr. Battle: (front row, left to right) Gilford Tolson,
Cynthia Douglas, Yvette Cottman, Phyllis Ervin, Mr. Battle,
Julia Proctor, Audry Spriggs, Theodora Brown, Joan Johnson; (back
row, left to right) Marvin Hawkins, Carl Hawkins, Walter Savoy,
Glen Turner, Carlene Newman, James Walls, Bernice Bolden,
Roland Brown, LeRoy Butler, Barbara Parker, Silverene Johnson,
William Tolson, Clifton Oden, Marvin Turner. The current band
members, under the direction of Ms. Schwanda Smith,
are in the background.

Wilbert Hawkins, shown speaking at the music wing dedication in honor of LeRoy A. Battle, is a former Douglass High School teacher (October 2007).

Mr. Battle receives the Champion of Courage Award from the Honorable Kweisi Mfume.

Jim and Susie Proctor with grandchildren Darren, David, and Autumn. Jim is a Maryland state delegate, and Susie, a former Douglass High School Majorette. They are a very special family and LeRoy cherishes their friendship.

Part III

Music

Transition from Harlem to Brooklyn

I was 11-years-old when my mother and father separated, and I never understood why. My father and I did not have a close relationship because he spent most of his time taking care of the candy store. The end result of this situation was the move to Brooklyn by my mother and me.

My extended family was in Brooklyn, New York. I stayed with my aunt Roberta Roderick (Aunt Bert) at 1544 Fulton Street. The front two rooms of the street-level apartment contained a beauty parlor with four booths for operators (called beauticians), a shampoo area, a manicure area, and a place where combs, curling irons, and brushes were sanitized. We lived in two rooms attached to and directly behind the beauty parlor. Aunt Bert slept in the back and I slept on a portable couch that was rolled in after the shop was closed (more details of my family life are depicted in my first book, *Easier Said*).

During this time, I had to literally follow the gigs; I took my drums wherever and whenever I heard a drummer was needed. Older musicians told me that I had to make a name for myself and the quickest way to make connection with those who could help me was to start hanging out at the Rhythm Club, located at Seventh Avenue and 132nd Street in Harlem.

So my Saturday morning started following this pattern: I would arise early, take care of my morning toilet, eat a hearty breakfast, and pack up my drums. I would take the bass drum case in my left hand, my snare case in my right, and head for the 8th Avenue subway. Now the subway had a round turnstile door entrance only one person at a time could get through. My first time getting through was a horrible nightmare. I got stuck in there with my bass drum and snare drum case. After 10 minutes, two large crowds formed, one of those trying to get to the subway on one side of the entrance and those who got off the subway and were trying to exit to the street on the other side. Finally, the subway police arrived to see what was holding everything up. One look at me and a few choice expletives told me that I was in very big trouble. After 15 more minutes, a special truck rolled up and several uniform-clad men came to the turnstile, each carrying special tools. After another 20 minutes, the turnstile started leaning and the men held it while I egressed and started to make my way to the subway. One of the repairmen called me over and instructed me on how to navigate the turnstile with large packages. The secret was, they had to go through separately. I was immediately relieved when those first shouts of anger turned to cheers when I was released from the turnstile, and foot traffic started flowing again in both directions.

As I said, I had to follow the gigs no matter how far. The travel time on the subway from Throop Avenue in Brooklyn to 125th Street Harlem was approximately 45 minutes. From 125th Street, I took a cab to the Rhythm Club and spent the day hoping for a gig. I worked all gigs in Harlem from the Rhythm Club, but seldom did I get Manhattan gigs from Brooklyn.

When I was 17, I took a gig for the summer playing for a resort in Poughkeepsie, New York. The routine ran about the same as most summer resort gigs, namely, the combo had to play dance music in the casino from nine PM until midnight. This resort had about 15 guest cabins and one hotel centrally located. The cabins were situated in a semi-circle around the hotel and in front of all this was a beautiful lake. After dinner, guests would gather in the casino for the dancing period. At midnight, I would pack up my drums and follow the crowd to the local bistro in Poughkeepsie. It was there on a particularly hot night that I ordered a delicious BLT (bacon, lettuce, and tomato) sandwich accompanied by a very cold mug of Schaefer beer (my first taste of alcohol). The resort had a library on site. During the day, I would pass the time reading novels. I would check out the books from the literary cabin; I also took up target archery.

At the end of summer, I started gig hunting from Poughkeepsie. I made telephone calls to just about every club owner or agent in New York. I finally got hooked up with a group that was scheduled to play a week in Bridgeport, Connecticut. As luck would have it, they needed a drummer. The group consisted of seven pieces: bass, drums, piano, two trumpets, and two saxophones (alto and tenor). Our pay was 25 dollars for the week. We were to play at a well-known supper club.

Supper clubs were very popular at that time. The club featured dinner and dancing along with a floor show. There were two shows a night, with the first one starting at 10 PM and ending around 11 PM, and the second show starting at one AM and lasting until two AM.

The show package consisted of a Master of Ceremonies, who was usually a very good-looking light-skinned Black man with charisma to charm the crowd. He would float around the stage or, on special occasions, take the microphone among the tables, and croon to special ladies who would swoon to his lyrics. Then there was a lovely chanteuse who would sing tearjerkers like "Just My Bill," or "My Man." This act was followed by a smooth tap dancer who would mesmerize the patrons in the manner of Maurice Hines. The next act would usually be comedy; the performer would have a drink nearby and a cigarette that he puffed on while he thought of who else he could insult in the audience. The last act in the show was a very good-looking man with slicked back hair, dressed in a white tie formal tuxedo; he played the marimba using two and four mallets. In front of the marimba, he hung a large round clock with just a second hand. At the start of his act, he would tell the people that he could play "Flight of the Bumble Bee" in 60 seconds. Then he would start the clock hand moving by stepping on a button with his foot. His hands moved so fast, they seemed like a blur. With a flair and waving of his arms, he would hit the last note exactly as the clock hand stopped at 12. The band would play a loud chord to emphasize the moment.

Usually, as the week rolled on, I could see familiar couples who returned for dinner, dancing, and the show. Well, it was the custom then in show business to end the last show with an unexpected act or routine, one which would cause discomfort to one of the performers. On the Sunday evening before the final show, the band decided to put the marimba player in his place. You see, all week he was unfriendly; he wouldn't speak to you if you spoke to him. He was very "stuck-up," or as we band members said, "He acts like he was smelling his upper lip." Earlier Sunday, our piano player (who was very good at electronics) took the marimba player's clock and fixed it so that the second hand would "fast-forward." The result was that at the one show that day, when the marimba player started the clock with his foot, that second hand spun around that clock in a flash. Unaware, the marimba player was sailing along, while the audience laughed and howled. The player looked puzzled, but continued playing to a second hand stuck on zero. When he completed the song, he held both arms up triumphantly, and the audience laughed; oh how they laughed and waved their arms at the player!

When the emcee clued him in, that marimba player's face turned beet red and he stormed off the stage madder than a wet hen.

Serious Gigging

I started gigging seriously when I was 13 years old. Max Roach, Ray Nathan, and Ernie Stewart were exceptional drummers who were in high demand. But other good drummers were scarce in Brooklyn at that time, so I was able to keep busy.

Steady work for combos was hard to come by; the best way young aspiring musicians could get practical playing experience before a live dancing crowd was to play the gig on a percentage basis. This is the way it worked: patrons were charged one dollar admission at the door. The band and the dance sponsor would each have representatives to co-collect the money. At the end of the dance, the manager would pay the band the agreed-upon percentage from what was collected at the door. At the most, the band got 20 percent and the house got the other 80 percent. This meant that each band member received about five dollars for the night. We were young and, most importantly to our innocent minds, we were plying our craft, so we were happy with whatever we were given.

During these times in Manhattan, the society crowd gave private "after-hour" parties at their palatial estates in Long Island. Often, they would send a car we called a "searcher" around to bistros and clubs looking for groups. There was no haggling over fees; they paid what to us was enormous money for our services (averaging 50 dollars each). These parties usually would last until dawn. In addition to the cash we received, the family cooks would load us up as we were leaving. On many occasions, I found chunks of roast beef and/or halves of cheddar cheese wheels in my bag. The limos would take us back to the club. From there, we went our separate ways home. Getting home wasn't a problem for me, because the Eighth Avenue subway ran straight to my home station.

Sometimes, I would arrive at Throop Avenue around six AM. It was about this time that I would run into our neighborhood milkman. I would hail him and purchase a quart of chocolate milk, drinking most of it standing next to my drums. I must have looked pretty weird first thing in the morning, dressed as I was in a tuxedo and patent leather black shoes. I greeted the people headed to work while I was preparing to go home and sleep.

Boat rides were the gigs I most looked forward to playing in the summertime. Boats would leave from lower Manhattan and go up the Hudson River to Bear Mountain; some would continue up to Indian

Point, where patrons could rent motor boats. These boat rides were great money making affairs for churches or private clubs. The band never worried about food on these boat rides because all of the girls constantly brought fried chicken, soda, and so forth to the bandstand.

There was no greater thrill for a musician than to play for such a captive audience. Sometimes your boat going would meet another boat returning, and all railings would be crowded with people yelling and shouting at each other as the boats passed.

Bands often were made up of gang members who came from various sections. However, a truce was observed and respected by all gangs on the boats. One time, I recall, two gangs on the boat broke the truce and started rumbling. I want to tell you that I was really concerned. The crowd rushed to one side to escape the fight, causing the boat to list to one side. I wondered whether the boat would keep on rolling over!

The Young Communist League (YCL) in Brooklyn

On the world stage, in the mid-1930s, the United Soviet Socialist Republic (USSR) was considered the number one global enemy of the United States of America. During this period, when I was approximately 15-years-old, several musicians got together to form a loose swing-type group, which consisted of drums, trumpet, piano, tenor sax, and alto sax. We didn't sound too professional, but the spirit was there. We managed to play for percentages at the dances given by unscrupulous promoters. One promoter hired us to play at this "dump" of a hall for two weeks. We were to play two hours a day, Mondays through Fridays, starting at five PM and ending at seven PM.

The main high schools in the Bedford-Stuyvesant section were targeted. Prior to the start of opening day, boys and girls of all colors were hired to hawk the occasion and to hand out fliers.

Opening day came one April afternoon. The band was in place and, lo-and-behold, there was a line waiting to enter. The promoter took the microphone and welcomed everybody, then he spun around and signaled us to start playing. A joyous yell went up from the crowd, with potato chips plentiful and the soda "flowing" like wine. The floor was jammed, and most of the targeted Black boys were dancing with the White girls, which flew in the face of the rampant racism of the day. This activity was repeated everyday.

One day several White policemen showed up. I saw the promoter go to them and I think they were paid off, because that was the last I saw of them for the rest of the dances.

After the last dance, when everybody had gone, the promoter called the band together. He told us what a fine job we had done, then he paid us. We each received a grand total of 20 dollars all for two weeks' work, but that 20 dollar bill looked very large in 1936! He then said that the band did not get a chance to dance with the lovely girls, so we're going to have a private party just for the band. At that, he went to the record console, and put on a jump tune by Jimmie Lunceford. At that time, six or seven White girls ran into the room, grabbed band members, and we started dancing. When the jump record finished, he put on a slow drag and, once again, the girls got a band member and coaxed him on the floor.

This White girl said to me, "Boots, we can do this every day. Why don't you join our group?" Well by this time, my interest was more than piqued and I was ready to join anything.

After the slow drag, the girls pulled out white cards and pens. The card had the words: "I _____ agree to the terms of joining the Young Communist League." I, along with the other band members, signed the card. The promoter collected the cards and said that he would be at that place for two more days just in case any of us had friends who would like to come and join.

The next day, my uncle Clarence said to me, "Boots, are you familiar with this White guy who is going around getting Black children in the Young Communist League?"

I explained that I did know the fellow, and I told Uncle Clarence about the dance and how I signed the membership card to the YCL. Uncle Clarence grabbed my arm, marched me to his car, and literally threw me in the passenger's side.

When we arrived at the hall, he stormed into the reception area. There was the promoter at a table along with the bundle of application cards. The promoter put on his most beguiling face, but before he could say good evening, Uncle Clarence grabbed him by the collar. Through clenched teeth, he said, "Give me my nephew's card."

The promoter's eyes bugged out of their sockets, and he rasped, "I'll be happy to do so!" Then, with Uncle Clarence still keeping a death grip on his neck, he fumbled through and came up with my card.

Uncle Clarence tore that card into bits and said to me, "C'mon, let's go."

Boy Scout Competition

Areas of great competition existed in Brooklyn between the Boy Scout troops. This involved the drum and bugle corps, and subsequently, the drum majors of each Boy Scout troop. The outstanding Scout drum majors did not use the long formal batons adorned with gilded twine, tassel, and a silver-looking ball at one end. Rather, they preferred to use the small silver baton, about three and a half to four feet in length. These were very suitable for twirling and were easier to handle when they did the drum major's strut. A drum major's fame was measured in direct proportion to how fast he could twirl the baton around his body, through his legs, or how high he could throw and catch it.

Clarence Fleet was the drum major for Berean Baptist Church, Troop Number 119. Fleet, as he was called, was tall, bow-legged, and had a Hollywood smile. Fleet had large hands and when he twirled that baton, it was like a blur. Then, as the combined drums and bugles would break into song, Fleet would slide into his special strut. His back would be stiff and his feet would barely touch the ground. The crowd would go wild; ladies would scream. Fleet went on to become a local club performer, twirling two batons and balancing a chair in his mouth. We used to tease Clarence Fleet by telling him, "Fleet, you won't become famous until you get a girl to sit in that chair while you lift her as you twirl."

My troop's drum major was Eugene Graham. He could twirl a little but that wasn't his strength. Eugene was very formal acting. He did not put on a show, but he was a solid leader who could keep time and add dignity to the process. However, Gene could afford to be reserved because the Bethany Baptist Church's Drum and Bugle Corps, Troop Number 197, was the best. No other troop could outplay us.

The most honored and outstanding drum major was George Nixon of Troop Number 198, of Concord Baptist Church. George was a magician with the baton. His technique was such that his baton never seemed to touch his fingers, yet he generated such speed with so little effort. Then, the thrill of all thrills, George would send his baton hurtling up through space, two stories high, execute a few fancy steps, and catch the spinning baton right on the beat.

One competitive activity that involved approximately 15 drum and bugle corps of our council district was held at the Bedford Armory, in the Bedford/Stuyvesant section of Brooklyn during the summer of 1939. In preparation for this great event, my Troop Number 197 increased our time of practice from one day a week to three days a week two hours each evening. The bugler's lips were quite sore and we drummers raised numerous blisters on our hands.

Mr. Talbert, our scoutmaster, said that we had to toughen ourselves for the long haul.

As the time got closer, we would play nonstop for one hour. In preparation for this part of our practice, we would fold all the chairs in the church basement and march around the large rectangle, six abreast. This competition was very serious to us because we wanted bragging rights as the best drum and bugle corps in Brooklyn.

We knew our stiffest competition would come from George Nixon and Clarence Fleet, Troop Numbers 198 and 119, respectively. I also knew that in order to win, our Troop Number 197 had to do something unique. So I started mapping a new strategy in my head. I envisioned my drum section playing an earthy drum beat. Instead of our marching in straight files and columns, we would weave patterns to a "savage" beat, with our drums sounding like massive tom-toms. We would unhook our snares. I was quite excited and emotional as I explained this to Mr. Talbert. Then I added, "We could wear pith helmets in place of our campaign hats. That would complete the picture."

Mr. Talbert looked at me and smiled (I think he did all he could do to keep from bursting out with a laugh). Then, as he always did when he had to negate an activity or turn down a request, he took me aside and proceeded to explain why the plan would be excellent for entertainment, such as in a show at a fair, etc. However, the judges would be concentrating on the geometric patterns of our files and columns. In addition, we would be out of uniform with the helmets and we would be judged failures before we played a note. He further added, "If we are to win, we must do it with very precise marching and playing, all of which involves bugles held high, played in tune, and drums sounding crisp."

We did not have plastic heads then. Our drumheads were made from the skins of unborn calves. If the day was damp and rainy, the drumheads would be slack in the middle, no matter how hard one turned the tightening rods on the side. To counter this damp condition would make our drums sound very dull. I told Mr. Talbert about a passage I had read concerning the Swiss drummers who used heat to draw the drumheads tight. Consequently, we always carried a Sterno kit that we used even on sunny days. The heat from the flames gave our drums a very high, crisp, attention-grabbing sound when played.

I was disappointed that my idea was not going to be used, but I did understand why. However, I kept trying to think of something that would make us unique. "What to do? What to do?" I kept asking myself. One Saturday, the answer came to me as I was watching a movie with Jean Harlowe and Franchot Tone. I do not recall the title; however, one scene depicted a French drum and bugle corps playing at an airport, welcoming an arriving dignitary. I immediately blocked out the actors and words, and just concentrated on the music being played in the background. Boy, what a picture the corps made. White, woven silk cords were draped around the drums. Beautiful lanyards were hanging from the bugles and all players wore white gloves. Well, I stayed and watched the whole show again to make certain I did not miss what that corps did.

That evening I went home and, to the tune of "Taps," I made an arrangement that was catchy and yet dignified. Mr. Talbot said, "Yes, Boots, you take over and rehearse the group. Meanwhile, I'll see that we get the gloves and lanyards we need." Well, to put it mildly, I was a hard taskmaster. I yelled and got in the faces of all who did not raise legs or arms or play to my satisfaction.

Finally, the big day arrived. As we approached the Bedford Armory, we could see the huge crowd entering the front. As we went around to the performers' entrance, we saw our competition, Black and White drum and bugle corps, all practicing formations and playing. It was a cacophony of noise and excitement. I went to each of our buglers and tuned them up. I knew from playing in the bands at school that all instruments had to be in tune, not sharp or flat. I listened as each drummer rolled softly on the drumheads, and then I made slight adjustments on their tuning rods. An official came out and told us to file in and where to stand on the floor. There was no seating, except for the spectators, who were upstairs in the balcony.

The armory was dark and very imposing. All of a sudden, search-lights came on in all colors: red, blue, yellow, and white. Their shafts of light cut through the darkness and never stood still. The reviewing stand was all-aglow with gold and silver decorations. Above was a huge American flag gently curling in the breeze from a directed fan.The drum and bugle corps all looked resplendent. As it happened, our troop would be the last to perform. At a given time, the Scout Commissioner raised his hand and, in a few seconds, you could hear a pin drop. He introduced himself and the platform guests, including the Borough President of Brooklyn. The Commissioner then explained that each troop would have a total of seven minutes: two to get to the starting place and five to perform.

Previously, when we first unloaded outside the armory, both George Nixon and Clarence Fleet came over to needle us and our drum major Eugene Graham. They were twirling their batons and bragging about how they were going to play us in to the "dirt." Quietly I said to Eugene, "You may not be able to twirl like they do, Gene, but you just keep your head high, your back straight, and pretend you're that Bristol drum major I told you about.

I told Eugene and the group to watch and learn. When Troop Number 119 of Berean Baptist performed, you could see tall lean Clarence Fleet bend backward and almost touch the floor; you couldn't help but envy his deer-like antics as he worked the audience. George Nixon of Troop Number 198, Concord Baptist, literally brought the crowd to its feet when he threw his baton whirling up into the rafters, then spun around to catch it without missing a beat.

As group after group performed, the band members became more and more restless and fidgety. I told the drum major to have the buglers drain the water out of their instruments one more time. (They had already done this, but I needed to keep them occupied for a few more minutes.)

I checked my watch and finally there was only one minute remaining in the previous band's performance. I then told the buglers to attach their lanyards, the drummers to drape their drums, and for all to put on their white gloves. Immediately, we were transformed into a unit with which to be reckoned. One could tell by looking into our eyes that newfound confidence we had. When the spotlight played over our group, a different glow seemed to emerge.At last it was our turn. I told the judge that we would use all seven minutes to perform, which means we were adjudicated from the first note we struck—and how we did strike. Our color guard was tall and stately; Eugene, with his long, formal baton, raised it high and blew a whistle; our buglers played Da-Da-Da and our drummers answered: Boom – Boom – Boom.

We marched and played the full length of the floor, executed a synchronized column to the right, and ended up facing the reviewing stand beside the other troops. The audience members were on their feet whistling, yelling, and clapping. The officials in the reviewing stand were all laughing with joy at our performance. When we finished our last note, I told the troops to freeze and look straight ahead, and to ignore the perspiration that was streaming down all our cheeks.

When finally the Commissioner asked for and got the silence he wanted, he looked around and thanked all who participated. Then, in a very solemn voice, he asked the color guard of Bethany Baptist Church, Troop Number 197, to come forward. It all seemed to happen at once. I gave the signal for our drummers to play a catchy beat, as our color guard moved out, then halted in front of the reviewing stand. The color guard Scout dipped his flag towards the Commissioner, who hung the first place banner on the staff. Bedlam broke loose. Troop Number 197 was the best!

Bedford Dance Hall

In the Bedford-Stuyvesant section of Brooklyn where I grew up, one social activity that the Colored teens literally gave their souls to participate in during the 1930s was to follow Clarence Berry's swing band every Sunday night, during summer months, to Seagull Beach.

The Seagull Dance Hall was located right on Island Avenue, and lines to enter would start forming around six PM. This line itself was a social event. Many guys would send their pretty ladies from the Bedford-Stuyvesant section early so that they could get a better place in line. Then later, the boys would come, holding bags of fried chicken and soda, and take their place in line when called by their girlfriends.

At seven PM, the orchestra would open up with this thunderous, groovy beat, the gates would be raised, and the revelers would pass through to the dance floor, dropping dollar bills in the double-guarded baskets. The dance would last four hours. When couples got overheated from dancing, they could go to the entrance to get the back of their hands stamped. They then exited to the boardwalk and enjoyed the sea breeze.

At intermission, the relief combo would take over. I was the drummer, along with five other musicians. The floor would not be nearly as crowded as when the big band played. However, the main reason for the relief band was to form up a "jam session." This was the venue for new musicians, and there was no lack of energy or musicians very anxious to show off.

The other activity going on simultaneously with the Seagull Dance Hall was the Sunday Night dance at the Bedford Dance Hall. Now this dance hall was located on the corner of Fulton Street and Bedford Avenue. To get into the hall, you had to enter the building through a door adjacent to a new car dealership's door. You could always tell that dealership from the three huge, sun-bright windows. Each showcased a brand new Ford under colorful spotlights. They seemed to challenge you to find a speck of dust on them. As you entered the door to the dance hall, you had to climb a long narrow flight of stairs to the dance hall's entrance. The cost was one dollar per person, and the collector could barely keep up with the dressed-up couples pushing in.

At least once a month, I would be the drummer for the pick-up band. The manager would contact the individual musicians during the week. In this manner, he would not have to carry a regular band. There were times when he would pay each musician a different night's pay. For example, if the manager knew you were a beginning musician, he would just give you a few dollars. On the other hand, I knew what I was worth, so I demanded and got top salary, which would be 15 or 20 dollars.

One night, I arrived at the dance hall a little after the first band had begun playing. What I saw as I approached the door stopped me in my tracks. The rhythm upstairs was booming and the dancers were stomping. Downstairs, the huge panes of showcase windows were ballooning back and forth, and I just knew they were going to burst. Fortunately, if they ever did, I wasn't aware of it.

Malcolm X

I met Malcolm X in 1936, when I was around 17-years-old and had landed a gig playing with the Jack McGuire Band at Small's. Small's Paradise was a nightclub located in Harlem on Seventh Avenue. This club, along with the Lafayette, was one of the most popular sites frequented by Colored people.

Weekends were a blast there. Everybody including fast ladies of the night, politicians like Adam Clayton Powell, or famous entertainers like Bill Robinson (who was considered the Mayor of Harlem) made it a point to be seen there.

One Saturday night the band was playing in the lounge downstairs for a private party, when I noticed a crowd of people surrounding someone.

I heard the master of ceremonies call out, "He's here; Detroit Red is here."

A few minutes later, this strapping young man strode to the band-stand and said, "You musicians play good enough to be in Detroit," and everybody laughed. Detroit Red said to the head waiter, "Set the band up with anything they want." He then came around and shook hands, saying, "I love the blues."

Before he got back to a table, our band leader Jack said, "Play number 17," which was a "gut-bucket blues." It is important to know that Harlem was in the midst of the "Harlem Renaissance," which began around 1921 (the year of my birth), and ended around 1936 with the "Kresge Department Store Riots."

Such literary giants as Richard Wright and Zora Neale Hurston, and musicians like Duke Ellington, Earl "Fatha" Hines, Fats Waller, and Cab Calloway played in all the theaters like the Lafayette or the Apollo. All the great Colored artists lived at 555 Edgecomb Avenue, New York, New York.

The Cotton Club was in Harlem, but Colored people could not attend. However, the greatest Colored artist entertained—Lena Horne, who was at first a dancer in the chorus line there. All the great Colored musicians lined the clubs on 52nd Street, such as Billy Ecstine, Billy Daniels, Pearl Bailey, Ethel Waters, etc.

Harlem Nights

An accordion player named Jack McGuire called me one night to ask if I would come to Harlem to play a two-night gig on a Saturday and Sunday. I said sure, if the money was right. He said the gig would pay me 40 dollars a night and that he could give me five dollars more because I had to come from Brooklyn. I agreed, and he said for me to wear black and a bowtie. I was told that the gig was at Paddy's Bar, which was located on 125th Street. We would play from nine PM until two AM with a 20-minute break each hour.

That Saturday afternoon, I put on my "gigging" clothes, put my drums under each arm, caught the Eighth Avenue subway, got off at 125th Street, and made my way to Paddy's Bar and Grill. Walking there was very taxing; I had to go up a street with a sharp incline. At the crest of the street, I spotted a white globe over a doorway and windows with huge four-leaf clovers on them.

I went through the swinging doors and over to speak with the closest bartender. He nodded and pointed to a small platform in a corner, which was attached to the ceiling and wall. Around the platform was a thin wooden rail, and facing the front were three chairs. I started up the side stairs, and was lifting my drums over the rail when two more musicians came up behind me. Both were carrying instrument cases. I arranged my drums around me, and the other musicians introduced themselves as Harold Smith (tenor sax) and Jack McGuire (accordion). We were setting up and just talking when a large red-faced Irishman said, "Hi guys, I'm Paddy. Anything you want to drink, just lower this tray and then pull your drinks up. We just serve soda or beer to the band, no whiskey. Is that understood?"

We all nodded our heads in agreement.

"Fine," Paddy said. "I don't want no misunderstanding the other group playing here gave me a hard time." Then he said, "Showtime in five minutes," and left.

We got along swell together, and everything went smoothly until I heard loud cursing below, and before I knew it, there was a fight. Jack said, "Play harder and louder, Boots."

The crowd moved from one end of the bar to the other. It was a weird scene looking down on a fight and not having to duck or pack up, which is what happened in other club fights. Soon the restaurant bouncers took over, collared the ruffians, and literally threw them out the front door.

Jack said to the musicians, "Okay, let's settle back; play something cool and slow."

Triangle Inn, Quogue, Long Island

In the mid-1930s, I got a gig drumming for a combo that contracted for a weekend at the Triangle Inn, located at the very tip of Long Island in a township called Quogue. I was very excited to have such a gig because it said to me in plain language that I was a true professional musician.

We, the five pieces, met at the Grand Central Station and got acquainted with each other during the long four-hour trip. Harold (tenor sax), Cliff (trumpet), Juancito (piano), and Little John (bass) were all older than I was; they had more experience, so I was very content to listen and learn.

When we arrived at the Triangle Inn, there was barely enough time to wash up, eat, and change into our jackets, which were provided for us by our leader Cliff. Most leaders carried a set of uniform jackets, which at that time were all too large for me. Cliff then passed out a few charts, saying, "We'll open each set with number one encircled with blue marker."

At this time, the people were crowding in. They jammed right up to the stage platform, which was built about two feet off the floor. Above the band were klieg lights of several colors, and there was a rotating crystal ball in the ceiling in front of the band, which was highlighted by several small spotlights. All of the lights were activated by someone behind the bar.

We struck up a jumping opening selection and, as soon as we hit, couples went to the floor. The crowd in front soon started rocking to Harold's soulful tenor solo. Cliff said to us, "We're going to play this like it was a regular dance." That is, we only took a 10-minute break each hour, and then we took a 30-minute break. That left only one hour for the gig that we swung right out.

This was a fine gig; there were no fights during the dance and the manager gave us all the food and soft drinks we wanted. Our sleeping quarters were small, but adequate. We were assigned two rooms of the Triangle Inn, which was an actual functioning inn. People came by car and train to reside there.

The band ate in the dining room with the guests. Afterwards, we strolled to the beach and I was surprised when the local townspeople pointed to the buildings across the bay and told me what I saw was Connecticut.

On the Road: New York State

One weekend, as our gig ended at the Three Deuces on 52nd Street, an agent came up to us as we, the Tony Scott Five, were packing. He went over to Tony (who played clarinet) and, after they huddled for a few minutes, Tony called the group over. They told us about a gig the agent had for us, in a town called Pawling in upper New York state. He said the gig would be for two nights at a nearby club, just a stone's throw from the train station. The terms, including pay, were fine from my point of view. He said the initial two nights would pay the sidemen 200 dollars, and that the agent would pay for two meals each day plus lodging. He added that, if the people really dug us, he would pick up on the option and extend the gig for five nights.

Later that morning, we were on our way. When we reached Pawling, the agent drove us to a house in the country. He told us this was where we would lodge. As we exited the cars, I could hear a loud thumping, along with music coming from the rear of the house. When we went upstairs, I glanced back downstairs. I saw a crowded open room, a small bar, and couples dancing to the music of a small combo.

We settled in two rooms immediately above the party rooms downstairs. The agent urged us to hurry up and change into our uniforms because the first show would begin in an hour. We scurried downstairs, looked in to see the partygoers, and laughed to ourselves, because we would shortly be part of a similar scene.

Things went great at the club. The manager was pleased because the dance floor was filled for each song we played, and there was plenty of applause after each dance. The floor show also was well received.

At the end of the night's gig, we were shepherded back to our sleeping quarters. It was eerie, as all was quiet. The lights and crowd were gone, and we tried to tiptoe quietly up to our rooms so as not to disturb anyone.

I was the last to shower and prepare for bed. Because my room's door to the hallway was slightly open, I took the doorknob and started to shut the door. Then I noticed a dim red light coming from a door cracked open across from mine and, as my eyes adjusted, I saw the tenants in the rented room across the hall.

There in the dim red light was a tall naked Black man standing in a large regular washtub in the middle of the floor. My eyes nearly jumped out of my head when I saw two comely brown-skinned beauties bathing this muscular man. One lady was washing his front and her washcloth did not neglect any part where I could see. The other lady had a pail of water that she poured over the standing man. In a few seconds, he stepped out, and both ladies started drying the man off. At this point, I closed my door, and awakened my roommate, who explained to me that those people were plainly just a pimp and two of his stable. I was really getting a reality lesson.

Surrounded by Racism at Camp Lakeland

In 1939, I was asked to be the drummer in a five-piece combo group that was scheduled to play in the summer up at Camp Lakeland, located in Duchess County, in upstate New York. This was my first professional trip, necessitating my being away from home for more than two weeks at a time. My salary was 18 dollars a week, and the perks were excellent.

The band had a cabin all to themselves and we were free the whole day. We would get three meals a day and all we could eat. I took up archery and row boating, and I had time for my love of reading. We only had to play for the social dancing in the casino for two hours, from eight PM to 10 PM. The casino closed at 10 PM, and then the guests would give campfire parties, to which the band was always invited. At these affairs, hot dogs were roasted, along with marshmallows, and beer and soda were plentiful.

Many of the guests were from the garment center in Manhattan. Through their union, many were given free vacations for a week. Now I don't know how long this camp had been functioning, but I was told that Duchess County, at that time, was a hotbed for the Ku Klux Klan. There were many Negro and Jewish people who worked for, or held offices, in the garment union. To me, it was a pleasant, satisfying sight to see every aspect of the camp integrated. At the social dancing times, many mixed couples danced to our music.

Each night there was entertainment at the casino, which would start immediately after supper. Upwards of 300 patrons would enjoy Broadway stars and plays from the Jewish Theatre of Manhattan. Our band would provide the music for the vocalists. Early one morning, around three AM, this quiet, bucolic setting was interrupted by the shrill, piercing sounds of a host of fire engines. I ran outside our cabin and saw the sky lit up with angry flames engulfing the casino. The air was heavy with hot acrid smoke. It was difficult to breathe. It soon dawned on me that my drums had been lost in that fire. I sat down on the grass and wept. Soon there were arms around me and hands on my shoulders. Low voices tried to comfort me. I did not know what to think or do, so I sat there until dawn. Oscar Smith, the leader of the combo, told me that the fire marshal had found a burned can of kerosene. The fire had been deliberately started.

Later that morning, I was on my way to the dining room for breakfast when one of the guests called to me and stated how sorry he was about my drum set. The other band members had smaller instruments that they had taken to the cabin when they finished playing. The guest put his arm around my shoulder and handed me an envelope. He informed me that the guests had taken up a collection, which amounted to 300 dollars. Now, I am not one who is subject to crying; however, this brought tears to my eyes again. I hugged him, and just then the camp car pulled up beside us, and the driver said, "C'mon, Boots—we're going to 120 West 48th Street, to Manny's, to get you a fine, new drum set!" The sunrise over Camp Lakeland to me was like a phoenix rising from the ashes.

52nd Street

One Sunday evening about 11 PM, I received a call from bassist Junior Raglen; he wanted to know if I was available to take on a steady gig at the Three Deuces on 52nd Street starting the next day. The pay would be 90 cents a week (musicians' talk; that was $90). I privately thanked the Lord and said, "Yes!" Now this was my first gig in a place recognized by all musicians in America and Europe as the Jazz Mecca. It was the home of such musical giants as Dizzy Gillespie, Coleman Hawkins, Charlie Parker, and Max Roach, just to name a few.

Playing at the Deuces was fast, on-the-job training for me. To begin with, the numbers were called and played in rapid succession. Usually, at a regular dance or wedding, after a selection was played, there was a lot of lollygagging among the musicians. Maybe two or three minutes passed before the next number was played.

On 52nd Street, a set consisting of six or seven selections was agreed upon. After each, the leader would exchange remarks with someone or explain something about the upcoming tune, and then stomp-it-off (this took about one minute). Many times during the night, the leader would invite a special musician or vocalist in the audience to stand and be recognized, or to come up to the stage and sit in for a few songs.

Playing on 52nd Street was truly an earth-shaking experience for me. Next to the Three Deuces was Club Downbeat, next to that was the Spotlight Club, and across the narrow street was the Onyx Club. All of these clubs had jazz greats headlining the show, each fronting a small swinging combo. You just cannot imagine what a thrill it was to be in the company of headline and international musicians and singers.

Between sets, the musicians would hang outside of the club, go to dressing room areas, or go to Pat's Bar on the corner. I remember strolling into Pat's when tenor man Don Byas called me over to join a group in a booth. When I got there, you could have knocked me off my feet. There was tenor saxophone great Ben Webster extending his hand to me. I couldn't help but notice his tie clasp. It was two inches in length and about one inch wide, encrusted with very small diamonds and, in the middle, with larger diamonds, were the initials B.W. The clasp had a small diamond chain attached to both ends. I vowed to get me a tie clasp like that someday.

Transition to Baltimore

It was one night while playing at the Three Deuces that my future in Maryland was foreshadowed. I was drumming with the Derrick Sampson Trio. Derrick was on piano and Oscar Smith was the bassist. One night while we were playing, Oscar leaned over and told me that he was going to leave the group and take a position in the music department at Morgan State College in Baltimore, Maryland. Later, during the break, Oscar laid it out on the table for me. He was taking a position as head of the music department. Now Oscar was quite a learned musician, college and conservatory trained, and he had played in Europe and so forth. He said he would like to put a lot of his theories into practice regarding college curricula in the field of music. At that time, I was enrolled at the Juilliard School of Music, so Oscar and I had some very interesting, enlightening talks about music. We exchanged ideas and very often both of us would compose selections proving a particular point.

Finally, the time came and Oscar left New York for Morgan. Our exchange of ideas had served as fodder for my musical growth, and I truly missed him. However, after seven or eight months, Oscar sent me a telegram explaining his difficulties with the percussion section. He asked me to come down and give him a hand. Now the percussion section is composed mainly of the following: snare drum, bass drum, cymbals, bells, xylophone, tom-toms, castanets, tambourine, and tympani. All these instruments are important for certain sounds written in the score by the composer. In my opinion, the tympani are the most complicated and least understood instruments by budding percussionists.

Within two weeks, I packed my clothes and drums, and boarded the Pennsylvania Railroad train to Baltimore, Maryland. That school year, it did not take me long to settle in and get used to the role of student instructor as well as student. I gained quite a bit of respect among both students and teachers because of my skills with the percussion instruments. More importantly, my ability to connect with the students encouraged very good "give-and-take" sessions that accompanied each one-on-one teaching session. It wasn't long before Black high schools in the area got permission to send their percussionists for me to instruct, especially on the tympani.

Scarlett Country Club

It was while I was a student at Morgan State College in Baltimore that I officially came in touch with the unsavory element in Baltimore. I shared an apartment with a group of Morgan students at 2625

Francis Street. There were four of us boys who shared this apartment. Everybody chipped in to take care of living expenses. The landlady agreed to make breakfast for us during the week. However, we had to do our own cooking on weekends. My contribution was a very rustic baked bean casserole that I concocted on Saturdays. I got the recipe from my Aunt Bert. It was a simple dish and, for the most part, went as follows: two large cans of baked beans, one large onion chopped real fine, one half cup of brown mustard, one cup of dark syrup, one half cup of tomato catsup, and six or seven slices of bacon. These ingredients were all mixed together, placed in a baking bowl, and baked low for two hours and, *Voila!* That, along with some cornbread, would hold over four hungry college students for the weekend.

One Friday afternoon, there was a knock at the door. I opened it to see a large, dark man in coat and straw hat. "Good evening," he said in a thick West Indian accent. I invited him in and gestured for him to take a seat. He never took his hat off, but he introduced himself as "Scarlett." He said he was looking for a musician called Boots Battle.

I nodded and said, "You're looking at him."

He gave a large toothy smile and extended his paw-like hand, saying, "I need a band for my club this weekend and I'll pay you good money."

"Whoa, just a minute," I said. "What and where is this gig?"

He smiled and said, "Okay, okay, I'll slow down. I own a country club up in Frederick, Maryland. It's called Scarlett's Country Club. How many pieces are in your group?"

"Five," I said.

"Fine," he replied. "I'll pay each 50 dollars a night, and you as leader will get 75 dollars a night, plus free food and transportation. Take a look outside the window and check out your chariot."

I looked out the window and saw a black stretch limo. He continued, "Your band and instruments will be picked up here at exactly 10 AM Saturday morning. You will arrive at the country club by noon. You will start playing at seven PM until 11 PM both Saturday and Sunday. Your pay will be in cash. The band will have a cabin to rest, sleep, and change clothes. You leave to return here Sunday night at 12:30 AM. Any questions?" he asked.

"Yes," I replied. "Where is the contract?"

"No paperwork," he said. "I do everything with a handshake."

We shook hands and, as he closed the door, he said, "Nice doing business with you, Boots. See you tomorrow at 10 AM sharp."

I looked out the window and before the long, black chariot drove off, I was on the phone to the rest of the band to tell them of our good luck.

Saturday morning we were all packed and ready for Scarlett. The limo rolled up at 10 AM sharp and we loaded our instruments with very light hearts. Each of us had two short-sleeve white shirts to go with our black trousers and loafers. That was our uniform. The driver was flying low when we hit Route 40. About halfway there, a state trooper motorcycle policeman pulled us over. Naturally, I was very apprehensive.

"We work for Scarlett," was all I heard the driver say. With that, the policeman actually smiled and waved us on. All the eyes of the band looked at me and we broke into broad grins. "Wow," we thought.

As we pulled slowly through the white gates of the country club, a pretty hostess came up to the driver's side and pointed out the band cabin, which was situated in the woods near a single-car track. There were several cabins, all located close to the swimming pool; sitting on a slight rise was the main house. We unloaded our suitcases and picked out the bunks we wanted. After about 15 minutes, we got back into the limo, which took us to the main house.

Several male handlers gave us help with the instruments. "No!" a female voice said. "You're going to play in front of the pool cabin. Please place your instruments on that porch."

"Boy, what a classy place this is," I thought.

After we had set up, the hostess came by, driving a little cart. "Follow me fellows," she said. "We're going to the kitchen to feed you." There awaiting us was a long table filled with platters of fried chicken, biscuits, mashed potatoes, and country string beans. Our beverage was iced coffee, in which there was a large scoop of whipped cream. We ate like kings, or rather, starved peasants.

At six PM, Scarlett came to our cabin and said, "Try these on." On each arm he had bright red coats of all sizes. Boy, we were sharp looking!

At about 6:45 PM, the cars started rolling in. There were sports cars, limos, and roadsters with the tops rolled back. Each car held at least one beautiful lady. Cars came from all over Maryland and the District of Columbia. Scarlett catered to Blacks only; no White people were admitted.

The dining room was all aglitter; gourmet food was the thing. At one point all lights were dimmed and the waitresses paraded in with flaming crepe suzettes.

Dancing was in the area bordering the swimming pool. The music sounded absolutely beautiful in this bucolic setting, as the gentle sounds wafted over the countryside.

Trouble with Giggin' Around

I had just moved from Brooklyn and I hardly knew any of the musicians in the area. Though most of the musicians I dealt with were very honorable, there were some unsavory characters out there who just wanted to take advantage of you, even though they played music themselves. One experience comes to mind; this particular gig ended up being a nightmare for me.

I received a telephone call one evening where I was rooming. The voice at the other end said, "Hello, my name is Cole and I'm looking for a musician, a drummer called Boots."

"Yeah, that's me," I replied.

Cole said, "Boots, I've got a gig for five pieces at a roadhouse in Warrenton, Virginia." He continued, "I've got four pieces lined up and I just need a drummer. Are you interested?"

"Look," I said. "I'm a stranger in these parts and I haven't the foggiest idea where Warrenton is."

"Okay," Cole said. "The gig pays 50 cents and I'll take the band in my car.

"That's fine," I said, knowing that the best way to get known in a new city was to play as many gigs as possible with different musicians.

"Wear black," he said. "I'll pick you up Saturday at two PM."

The next day, I had my black suit, white shirt, and black bowtie on waiting on the sidewalk with my drums. At 2:15 PM, this big dirty car rumbled up beside me and a tall shifty-eyed black dude got out. He came around the motor, extended his hand, and said "Hey, I'm Cole," and we shook hands.

As I looked into his eyes, I truly did not like what was peering back at me. But we loaded my traps in his trunk and he said to climb in the front; there were four guys huddled in the back. Cole jumped in front behind the wheel and said, "Guys, this is Boots, our drummer. You all introduce yourselves; we'll be friends by gig time."

One fellow in the back said, "Man, you got any grass?" I didn't answer him, but thought to myself, this is just what I need, a bunch of dope addicts. And sure enough, after we left the city and were in the Virginia countryside, the guys lit up. They shut the windows and in a few minutes, the car was foggy with blue, acrid smoke. I cracked the window on my side because the marijuana smoke was getting to me.

"Shut that window," someone in the back yelled. Cole looked at me and said, "What's a matter, Boots?"

After a few minutes more, I rolled down the window and said, "I'm sorry, I don't smoke, and this smoke is bothering me. Stop the car and I'll get out now."

"Take it easy Boots," Cole said as he rolled down his window. "We're all friends and we do want a good sounding gig." We rode the rest of the way in silence, the only sound coming from the music playing on the radio.

There was an early group waiting as we rolled up in front of the hall. "Can I carry your drums?" some very young wannabe drummers asked.

"Sure," I said. Two boys grabbed the cases and struggled up the stairs. "Whatever you do, please don't drop those cases," I said.

After about 30 minutes, the joint was jumping, as Fats Waller always said. While we were playing, I noticed this fellow wearing a long back overcoat; this was in July. He would move from table to table, and finally, he was at the front of the bandstand. I saw a lady go up to this guy, and I saw him sort of hunch his shoulders as he opened his coat. You could've knocked me over with a feather. There were about five rows of half-pint whiskey bottles in his pockets, side by side, row on row. The lady was very busy looking over the stock. Cole came over to me and said, "Moonshiner."

After the gig was over, I started packing up when I heard two or three shots outside. Someone ran up to the band and said, "Your manager's been shot."

"Damn!" I thought. "What now?"

All the band members ran to the front. The police had some boy in handcuffs, and they were pushing him toward a police cruiser. An ambulance came, sirens and lights blaring. Paramedics worked their way towards Cole's body. After a while, they placed him up on a stretcher, loaded him in the rear, and sped away with lights and sirens blaring. The band members were all stoned, high on the weed they'd smoked during the drive up. I left them and went to the club's owner. "What happened?" I asked.

The club owner said that Cole was making a drug deal with a bad hombre from those parts. That guy was always in trouble and he always packed or carried a gun. Well, the deal fell through and Cole tried to "Bogart" the guy—meaning, he tried to bluff his way out and the guy pulled out his heat and blasted Cole.

I said, "Mister, the band is all the way down here from DC. How are we going to get home?"

The club owner looked around and called a guy over. Both he and the fellow huddled in private for a few minutes, and then the club owner said to me, "This fellow agrees to drive you to DC for a fee of 275 dollars."

There was no argument on my part. I went over to the band, laid it out on the table, and told them what the deal was—no if ands or buts. The ride back cost us a pretty penny apiece, and that was one expensive lesson for me to learn, to trust my instincts when dealing with people.

I found out several months later that Cole lived, but that he would never walk again.

Emory Grove in Montgomery County

It was in the late 1940s (before I was connected with the Altones) that I caught a gig with "Buddy and his Pals." This was the usual five-piece combo, which consisted of a singer, piano, bass, tenor sax, and drums.

The leader was a cat called Buddy. He was a typical "Latin Lover" type: tall, with wavy hair, a real ladies' man who sang and tried to play the bongo drums. The piano player was a very large dude called "Chink," because he had eyes that slanted. The tenor sax player was always sleepy-eyed from drugs. He could play, but his efforts were sporadic. He could start a good solo, but would fade away; I guess his brain was too scrambled. The bass player had a great driving beat, but he played the same changes no matter what key. I, the drummer, rounded out this motley group we called a band.

When I first arrived in Maryland and was attending Morgan State College, I took any and all gigs that came my way, because I wanted to learn who was who in the music business.

One night I was jamming in a club in Baltimore, when Buddy approached me and told me he was looking for a drummer to play with his combo. He further stated that he was booked for six weekends at the Emory Grove in Montgomery County. We were to play every Saturday and Sunday night at this place. The pay was 20 dollars a night. He also said that he would drive the band to and from the gig.

I agreed to his terms, and he told me where to meet him that coming Saturday (with my drums) in order to be picked up. That Saturday evening, I met him at the designated spot and he, along with the afore-mentioned band members, arrived in this large old touring Buick. Buddy introduced me all around to the members and we settled in for the long ride up to Emory Grove.

After about an hour, we hit a lonely stretch of dark road that wound up and down through wooded areas. Finally we started passing parked cars on both sides of this narrow road, and we pulled up in front of a barn-like structure. People were everywhere. Somebody yelled, "Here's the band!" Our car was surrounded with men and women yelling, "Hurry up, we didn't pay to look at the sky." After we unloaded, I made my way to the narrow bandstand. Somebody was plunking on the upright piano, and we had to chase them away so we could get set up. After awhile, we started playing, and soon the dance floor was packed. Buddy started singing the blues and the tenor sax player started wailing the crowd went wild. It was cold outside but perspiration was pouring off the dancers. Guys were going around bootlegging whiskey.

At about one AM, we came back from our break and started playing. "Where's Buddy?" I asked.

"Don't worry about him, " Chink replied.

After an hour went by, still no Buddy. About 2:30 AM, I heard a couple of gunshots coming from outside. A minute later, a man ran
through the crowd up to the bandstand and said, "I think Buddy will
be very late from this break."

"What happened?" I asked.

He replied, "Well, you know that state trooper who came here and
then went over to talk with the owner? He went to his cruiser and saw
a couple making love—the back door was open." He continued, "I
think it was Buddy. I never got a good look but the trooper fired two
shots at a fleeing figure going into the woods."

Fortunately, the "Latin Lover" had made a clean getaway that
night.

Buddy did show up at gig's end and was able to drive us home.

Another Gig at Emory Grove

Emory Grove was one of those joints that Hollywood writers like
to portray in films. The building was like an old barn, with tables and
chairs against the inside walls and a tight area for the dance floor.

There was an area set up for the bar, which consisted of four long
slats of wood about 16 feet each in length, 12 inches wide, and four
inches deep all pushed together to form a platform to serve the drinks
and food. These boards were held up by barrels on both ends and one
in the middle. Behind the three barkeeps (two women and one burly
man) lay a double-barreled shotgun on a table.

On weekends, the crowd came to this place to party. It was often a
very volatile situation. Anything could and would start an altercation.
Usually, the fights started over a contested lady. Sometimes, while
drumming, I could pick out when a fight was going to start.

I would watch a certain girl, usually one who had a certain way
with men because of her good looks and curvaceous body. This lady
would flirt with other guys even though they would be with their girl-

friends, and then the ladies would get into it. Or, in some cases, the men would have too much to drink and would try to take advantage of another man's girl. This would sometimes end up with a knife fight or worse, someone would start shooting. On many occasions, I would yell," Gun!" to the band. We would unceremoniously stop playing and jump behind the piano at the first shot.

The owner and his crew would break up the fight, evict the offenders, then get to the public address system to talk smoothly to the crowd. Then he would tell Buddy to play slow blues to get everybody dancing. The patrons were used to this—they did not panic and run to the exit, but I never got used to it.

The place never was closed because, actually, no one ever got killed. The fights never spilled to the outside, so it wasn't considered a threat to the community. Still, Emory Grove was a virtual cauldron of the unexpected.

One night it started to snow just as the band finished playing, and we started packing up to go home. I loaded my drums into the big car and climbed in the back, shivering and waiting for the rest of the band to come so that the heat would start and we could be on our way. As it turned out, Chink and Little John (bass) stumbled to the car, got in, and promptly fell into a drunken sleep.

The owner came to the car and said that he needed help to get Buddy to the car. I went back into the place with the owner and saw Buddy sprawled out on a table. The owner placed our night's pay in my hand, saying that Buddy was too wasted to do business. Together we lifted and carried Buddy to the car.

The owner looked at me, laughed, and said, "Well, Boots, it looks like you're going to be the chauffeur tonight."

"But I don't have license, I've never driven a car," I said.

"Look Boots," the owner said. "You're just going to have to suck it up and get this car to Washington."

I climbed behind the wheel (it seemed like a very large wheel), turned the ignition key, and just sat there while the motor warmed up. I didn't warm the motor on purpose, I was thinking, trying to mentally make my way back home.

Finally, I put the car into reverse and then pulled onto the main road. The snow was coming down heavier. I looked at the passed-out members, said a silent prayer, and pointed the car south.

I crawled along at 20 miles per hour, never doing over 30. When we reached Silver Spring, I was relieved to see that there was little or no traffic. Shortly, I saw flashing lights in the rear view mirror. I cursed out loud and pulled over, ever so slowly. A patrolman with a large flashlight shown it in my face and said, "Are you in trouble? You were going so slow, I thought you might need help."

"Hello Officer," I replied as respectfully as my scared body would let me. "No, I was just looking out for black ice."

He laughed and said, "No problem, the temp has risen a notch. Take care."

I thanked him and thanked my good Lord that he did not ask for my driver's license. By the time we got to our meeting place, I was able to arouse Buddy, give him the money, and bid farewell. That was the last gig I played with him.

Doe-Doe

One guest musician who used to sit in when we played at Emory Grove was a tall, carefree acting dude who played a mean alto sax. He was the house favorite and a darling of the ladies. The only name I know that he went by was the one the girls called him, "Doe-Doe." "Play that sweet horn, Doe-Doe," they would say when they would crowd around the bandstand.

Doe-Doe was really cool. He wouldn't let the sweet talk faze him. Many a night I would call his attention to some hot looking chick who was giving him the eye. Doe-Doe would say in a nonchalant manner, as he waved his arm in a negative way, "Man, forget that chick. If you want her, take her." He followed up with a laugh in my direction.

To this day, I don't know just what became of Doe-Doe. I assumed we would meet on gigs, etc., but we never did.

"Little Willie"

At this point in time, the most powerful character in Baltimore Black society was a gentleman known as "Little Willie." Now Little Willie, it was rumored, was in charge of the entire numbers racket. He was a giant in real estate where Colored people were concerned. He owned, or had a hand in, all of the Black night clubs; the aforementioned Scarlett was in Little Willie's control.

In spite of these nefarious dealings, Little Willie basked in the sunlight of respectability. His accountant was rumored to be the renowned Bert Parks, of Parks' Sausage fame. Bert Parks had a sister who was a truly gifted musician and band leader. She fronted a talented group of ladies in an all-girl orchestra. This group could out swing the average professional male band. They were on equal par with that famous group of female musicians from Harlem known as the "International Sweethearts of Rhythm." Parks' Sausage was very popular among all races and sold in all the major chain stores on the east coast.

For some reason, the Parks' company ran into very deep financial difficulty and was scheduled to go out of business. I know my family did not want this to happen; those red and white soft packages in the meat section contained delicious sausage that served well for breakfast, lunch, or any meal any time. It was rumored that Franco Harris, fullback for the Pittsburgh Steelers, was in the market to purchase the Parks' business.

During this era, Baltimore was alive and jumping. All the clubs were doing great—crowds gathered at the Sportsman Club, Gamby's, and Club Astoria (just to name a few). Famous stars, such as Red Foxx, Cab Calloway, Billy Eckstein, etc., made weekends heavenly.

It was my good luck to play with combos who did the after hours gigs. We would play at houses rented by Little Willie and his group for very special functions. The holiday parties were the greatest, because all the nightlife people attended: chorus girls, big-time gamblers, pimps and their cohorts, lawyers, doctors, and certain policemen.

In the serving area, long tables were assembled, made of several four- by eight-foot plywood pieces placed end to end and covered with special cloth imprinted with seasonal designs, like Christmas trees, snowflakes, sleighs, etc. Starting at one end, a server handed out the Parker House rolls from a lined four- by four-foot bin filled to the top. Next was a server slicing from a whole baked ham. Next to him was a server carving from a steamship round of beef. Next to him was a server doling out southern fried chicken. The table ended with black-eyed peas, greens, gravy, and mashed potatoes. Another section of the room had a station for all the bottles of alcohol, with ice, cherries, etc.

Downstairs was the on-going "Craps" game. It was a very noisy section and one could hear "Bet one grand, two grand ..." Next was a set of tables (five each) where "Spit-in-the-Ocean" was played, and 100 dollar bills flowed like wine. Upstairs on the third floor were special rooms for those who came from out of town.

The evening would begin around 10 PM; the band would set up in an open two- or three-room section. Special dance floors were also put down. Our band would start playing at 10 PM and play continuously until daybreak. Musicians took breaks only one at a time because there had to be continuous music. Each player got one thousand dollars at the end of the gig.

As a drummer from New York, I was very popular with the bands; they liked my "Gotham-beat." The soloists felt that they were playing more intensely when I backed them with my drums.

My favorite place to gig was the Club Astoria on Edmonson Avenue. This club had a circular bar where the band set up inside the circle. The platform was at eye level with the patrons and the musicians looked down on the customers. Now when we played, you couldn't help but catch the eyes of interested patrons. One time, one comely lady caught my eye. The cashier tapped me on my leg and said, "That young lady would like to buy you a drink."

I said, "Eggnog." Well by night's end, I had consumed over six eggnogs and my head was swimming. I could hardly keep the beat, so the leader of the combo took pity on me and got a guest drummer to complete the last set. I passed out and "Pigmeat," a fellow musician, took me home. I never found out what happened to the young lady who so generously plied me with eggnog, but one thing I did learn from that experience was to have my eggnog without alcohol.

As a new drummer in Baltimore, I had the good luck to play with many good combos: Pigmeat, who played a mean tenor sax; Flink Johnson, who acted a little on the hip-swaying side, but he was a fabulous entertainer on vocals and organ; Johnny Sparrow and his Bows and Arrows who carried such a down home funky beat; and there was the always cool and classy group, "3 Bs and a Honey."

Many times during the 1950s, I would be called to fill in for groups that came from out of town. Most of the time, I was called to fill in for a drummer needed at Sparrow's or Carr's Beach. Both of these beaches were very, very crowded on the weekends, solely because Blacks could not attend beaches like Sandy Point, or go dancing at the Spanish ballroom located at Glen-Echo. Like I said, Saturdays were busy, but Sundays were the big name day.

Playing at Sparrow's or Carr's beaches reminded me of my gigging in Manhattan on the marvelous Hudson River Day lines, where we would play for picnics on boats sailing up to Bear Mountain or Indian Point. But the greatest thrill for me was to be able to play drums and backup such performers as Ella Fitzgerald, Pearl Bailey, Bobby Blue Bland's Band, etc. It just seemed that all of Baltimore and the surrounding areas were jumping with live music, with such music combos as Johnny Sparrow and his Bows and Arrows, Pigmeat and his tenor sax, Henry Baker and his tenor sax, Buck Hill (well-known sax man), along with keyboard artist Tee Carsons.

Meanwhile, a group of musicians (some like myself attended Morgan State College) formed a group called the Mo-Bops. We were very popular and played the local college dances for both Blacks and Whites. Also, we played at several taverns and night spots, like the Fulton Street Tavern, where we backed blues singer Piney Brown. The members of the Mo-Bops were Monty Poulson (bass), Charles Baskerville (piano), Flash Gordon (mandolin), and Walt Dickerson (vibraphone), whose cousin sang with the Mariners Quartet that appeared daily on the Arthur Godfrey radio program.

Swingin' at Glen Arden Hall

Glen Arden is a little township considered a suburb of Washington, DC. It is a quiet place whose dwellers are all Colored. It is a fast-growing neighborhood with many new cottages.

The main place for entertainment there was Glen Arden Hall, a two-storied, white cinderblock, rectangular building. Our band, the Altones, played gigs there regularly. The gig would start at 10 PM and the crowds were overwhelming. The band would set up on the second floor, and you really had to get there early to occupy a table. All of the beer and whiskey was bootlegged. This was one busy joint and, I might add, dangerous, because fights broke out at any time. Thankfully, there wasn't much gun play.

Those groups who were unfortunate, and could not enter because the joint was overcrowded, would start dancing outside. The town police discouraged this because it jammed the entrance and prevented evacuation in the event of an emergency.

Saturday nights at Glen Arden were truly the Black young adults' social event in that area of town. Youth gangs set up headquarters around certain cars. Scantily dressed young ladies entered the hall together; sometimes one girl would shake her behind to answer a rude remark made by a gang member.

R.W.L. wine was passed around for all to take a swig. To the gang bangers, R.W.L. meant "Run, walk, and lay down."

The Crownsville Gig

In 1951, The Altones received a call from the superintendent of Crownsville State Mental Hospital. He stated that one of his staff members had recommended our group for this particular affair. In short, he wanted the Altones to play a graduation party for a group of hospital patients. He told me to contact Ms. Betty Stathem for the particulars.

Betty was a music major like myself and we both were recent graduates of Morgan State College. I just couldn't imagine what Betty, the hospital, and the Altones had in common. Boy, was I in for a very unique experience, to say the least. I called Betty that same day, and she said for me to come to the hospital the next day at noon so we could lunch together. The following day I made my way through the imposing entrance to the hospital grounds and asked the first person in a white uniform for directions to the employees lunch room. Betty was there at the door to greet and escort me to the table she had set aside for us. After we stood in line to get our trays, we moved quite rapidly though the food line. The selections were very appetizing—I chose fried chicken, baked potato, green peas, a roll, iced tea, and a slice of pie.

All during the meal, we did not talk about the gig but rather we relived the good and bad times we both experienced at Morgan. After eating, Betty showed me to another large room in the same building. She said, "Boots, next Saturday afternoon from one to four PM, we want you to play for the graduation party of those patients whose mental recovery will permit them again to enter society and function socially." She continued, "Many of the patients have made tremendous strides to this level where they can relate on a non-threatening basis with others. They will be seated cabaret style at tables, three couples to a table. They will be dressed in their Sunday best; they really are looking forward to wearing something besides the regular hospital clothes. It was very interesting to hear them call home and describe what suit or dress someone should bring. For them, this meant matching shirts, ties, socks, and shoes. I had to have many sessions with them individually and in groups at the beginning planning stages of this affair. We had to gradually mix the ladies and men by getting them to do tasks together, such as decorating, or painting signs that were put up in dorms and hallways advertising this event."

Both men and women asked each other out as dates. Family members were invited and menus were decided upon—no liquor or beer, the only drinks allowed were soda or punch. The kitchen staff prepared potato salad, cold cuts, rolls, and desserts.

Saturday afternoon finally arrived. I had the band arrive at 11 AM. We set up and talked with some of the staff. At one PM sharp, the patients started coming in. Betty announced over the public address system that it was open seating, only six at a table. All of the people were really dressed for the occasion. Some ladies wore really dressy evening gowns. Their hairdos were gorgeous, with lots of afros for both men and women.

Before we hit a note, Betty asked the band to play very soft and soothing selections. She asked me, the drummer, not to have any loud crashes on the cymbals or bass drum. She also asked that we not play anything too up tempo, like "Running' Wild."

When the lights were lowered, I told the band to lead off with "I Love You," and I did not use my drumsticks. Rather, I produced a soft sound with my brushes. We segued from one selection right into another, this to keep a mellow background. We followed the first number with "Singing in the Rain," then "Begin the Beguine." The dancers were doing a light fox trot or slow drag. At the end of the set, some couples applauded and some gathered around the bandstand.

Throughout the dance, many individuals (men and women) danced by themselves.

The afternoon proved to be very interesting to me, and the saying, "music soothes the savage breast," took on a new significant meaning for me.

Exchange Program with Bates High School

One of the most satisfying on-going relationships I had during my tenure at Douglass was with the Bates High School Band in Annapolis, Anne Arundel County, Maryland. Wiley H. Bates High School was the only high school for Colored students in Anne Arundel County until 1966. The band was under the most able direction of William Reid. It was in the mid-1950s that Bates and Douglass started having their bands give exchange concerts.

In the meantime, Bill and I struck an agreement that allowed for Bill to give both private and sectional woodwind lessons to my bandsmen, and I would reciprocate by giving percussion instruction to his drum sections. I knew that the Douglass students were very fortunate, indeed, to have extra lessons from Bill, because he was, without a doubt, the finest woodwind teacher around. In addition, Bill was well connected with the bands who played for circuses and who played backup for famous singers when they came to town.

Our first appearance at Bates was in October 1954. It was at a half-time show of a football game between Bates and one of their archrivals. My students really got a big kick out of performing beside the Bates High School Band. It was a new experience for them because Douglass, at that time, did not have a tackle football team.

That following spring, Bates High School gave a magnificent concert at Douglass. I recall one of Bill Reid's advanced music students, T. Arthur, who rendered a very fine flute solo. In addition, the Bates Band played an original selection written and arranged by T. Arthur.

There is another part of Bill Reid that I would like to call to your attention; another reason why I admired the man. It was around 1962 that the Annapolis Chapter of the National Association for the Advancement of Colored People (NAACP) called for a "sit in" of a local restaurant that refused to serve Negroes. Bill Reid, along with seven or eight teachers and students from Bates High School, entered this restaurant and sat down, prepared to give their food order. The owner, instead, demanded that they leave, but Bill and the others refused. At this point, the owner turned a fire hose on them with full pressure. The police were summoned and, in the end, the group left. However, they did strike a telling blow against segregation.

Concert at Delaware State College

During my tenure at Douglass, our band took trips to many cities, including Fairfax, Virginia; Charles County; Rockville, and Coney Island, New York, etc. However, the one trip that made an everlasting impression on me was our trip to Delaware State College.

I met James L. Hardcastle in April 1962. I was introduced to him when he paid our family a visit. He was principal of William Henry Middle School in Dover, Delaware. He and my wife's sister had attended Bowie State College together. Mr. Hardcastle had heard quite a bit about my Douglass Eagle Concert and Marching Bands; consequently he "cornered" me and talked music curriculum with me for quite a few hours. Then an idea popped into his head, "Would you and your band be willing to come to Delaware State College and render a concert?"

I replied, "Before I could give the go-ahead on that, many questions would have to be answered satisfactorily, such as: What day and time? Where would we stay (we're talking about 100 students)? What about meals (supper, breakfast, lunch, etc.)?

Our conversation continued. The concert would be held at Delaware State College in their auditorium. Mr. Hardcastle assured me that even though the regular students would be on their summer break, he could guarantee an audience of town parents, summer school students, and local church members. He stated that his school would fund all of our expenses including three Greyhound buses, all meals, and any cost incurred while stopping at the various fast food places enroute.

After we set the date and time (a Sunday in July starting at seven PM), I wrote everything up, made a copy, and told Mr. Hardcastle I would get back to him after I had conferred with my principal, Mr. Robert Frisby, and the Douglass High School Band Boosters Club. After two weeks of intense meetings, I got the positive response for which I was looking.

The band would be housed in college dorms, with all females on the third floor, three to a room. The female chaperones would stay two to a room at both ends of the hall and in the middle. The same went for the male bandsmen, who would be housed on the first floor, with the male chaperones having rooms near the staircases and elevators. In the meanwhile, Mr. Hardcastle was hard at work getting the newspapers, which ran pictures of the Douglass Band along with interesting articles, to pique the curiosity of the general public. In addition, announcements were read in churches and flyers were strategically placed in the windows of prominent businesses around town.

A few days prior to the trip, we had a joint meeting with my principal, Mr. Frisby, the entire Concert Band, and the Band Boosters Club. Everybody was encouraged to offer suggestions about informal dress for going and returning, and small bags for personal items (toothbrush, combs, brushes, deodorant, etc.). The three bus drivers reminded all (students and parents) that no smoking would be tolerated. I then told everybody that the cleaners would be in that week to collect and clean the uniforms. Every uniform would be spic and span and hung in new garment bags.

On Sunday morning at five AM, we met at the school to load our instruments and board the buses. There were 15 chaperones in all (male and female) to cover the three buses. There was no seating order; students could arrange to be with their own groups. After everyone was seated, I took still photos of the occupants of each bus (using our new Polaroid land camera). Everybody was advised that they had to sit in these same seats for the return trip (thus assuring an accurate count).

The Band Boosters provided stocked soda coolers for each bus, and there were ample sandwiches and potato chips. We arrived at Delaware State College some six hours later and there was a smiling welcome committee to greet us. The students were shown to their rooms and given free time to freshen up, relax, and watch television.

At two PM, all were called over the dorm public address system to come to the refectory for brunch (dress for this was informal). The guides led us to a building close by, where the wonderful aroma of hamburgers and hotdogs permeated the air. Each person picked up a tray and eating utensils as they headed for the various food stations. In addition to the meat entrees, there were French fries, baked beans, potato salad, cold cuts, rolls, and iced tea. Mr. Hardcastle introduced the cafeteria manager and workers, and told us that they volunteered to feed us. Immediately the band cheered loudly, which brought wonderful smiles to those who helped; we did let them know how much they were appreciated.

I then made an announcement that, after eating, all band members were to go to their rooms, change into uniforms, and report to the stage with instruments by 4:30 PM. This would give them ample time to take care of their personal needs, relax for about 15 minutes, and then be ready for business. At 4:30 PM sharp, the band started filing in.

With the assistance of the volunteers recruited by Mr. Hardcastle, I had arranged the chairs in concert formation.

I called all of the first chair musicians together and had them tune up to B flat by our oscilloscope. It was then up to them to see that their individual sections were tuned. At six PM, I asked Mr. Hardcastle to see that the stage curtain was closed. Soon, I peeped through an opening; I could see and hear the audience filing in. At 6:30 PM, I told the band to go to the restrooms and "empty their tanks." However, they must be seated and ready to go by 6:45 PM.

I then told them they could softly warm their instruments up by playing scales, etc. (this also helped to work off anxiety and nervousness). At seven PM, the auditorium lights went out and the stage lights came on. There was tapping on the microphone by the announcer, who said, "Ladies and gentlemen, we are privileged this evening to hear one of the best concert bands in Maryland, which is led by an outstanding conductor in the person of Band Leader LeRoy A. Battle." The announcer then went on to give accolades to the band and with that, the curtains slowly opened and I was very happy to see, as I squinted out over the blinding footlights, a very crowded auditorium. The applause was thundering; vaguely in the background I heard, "I now give you Mr. LeRoy A. Battle and the Frederick Douglass High School Eagle Band." I then bowed, stepped up to the microphone, acknowledged Mr. Hardcastle, the Band Boosters Club, and then announced the opening selection: Richard Wagner's "Die Meistersinger." The concert was a huge success; we played three encores. Afterwards, the stage was crowded with patrons anxious to meet our players.

After the concert, Mr. Hardcastle had arranged for a dee-jay to entertain the band in the dorm's recreation room. After changing my attire, I was escorted by several Delaware State instructors to a local club where the welcome mat was put out for me.

When I returned to the dorm, I was met by several members of the band, who insisted that I check each room on the first and third floors.

No one was asleep; all were in bed yakking about the good food and fun they were having.

The next morning, the loudspeaker sounded off at seven AM, informing students that their breakfast would be served at eight AM. This would give them ample time to shower, dress, pack their belongings, and meet at the bus at 7:45 AM. After stowing their belongings on the bus, they could then file into breakfast at eight AM. We were greeted with a wonderful array of food: flapjacks, sausage, eggs, cantaloupe, orange juice, milk, etc. After breakfast, I called all of the cafeteria volunteers to the center of the room and presented them with a huge bouquet of flowers, as thanks from the Douglass Concert Band. At 10:30 AM, we were all seated and ready to head home to Upper Marlboro, Maryland.

As a wonderful off-shoot to the concert, Douglass senior musicians who so desired were given full scholarships to Delaware State College as instrumental music majors. Delaware State's Director of Music had attended the concert and was extremely impressed with the musicianship of our senior bandsmen. Altogether that first year, Dr. Rhepert Stone awarded five full scholarships to the Douglass Bandsmen.

The Delaware State College Trip/Concert proved to be a wondrous life experience for the Douglass Eagle Band. Many lessons were learned that would benefit the students eternally. Scholarships were earned, demeanor was the "buzz" word, and respect for authority was seriously practiced. For all of the above, I salute our benefactor, Mr. James Hardcastle, whose foresight made it happen.

Joseph Ennis' Drill Team

When I was a member of the marching band at Morgan State College, I was always impressed with the showmanship and reception received by the Reserve Officers Training Corps Drill Team that marched directly behind the band. At that time, I made a promise to myself that, when I became a high school band director, I would definitely have a drill team that would be included in the line of march directly behind the band. In the early 1960s, the opportunity to organize a drill team came when the Douglass "A" Band purchased new parade/concert uniforms. I knew exactly where the old uniforms should go. The term "old" is actually a misnomer, because all of the "old" uniforms were really in pretty good shape.

I broached the subject with Joseph Ennis, who was a truly dedicated, and effective mathematics instructor at Douglass, and a proven champion for the students. I asked Joe if he would be willing to organize and train a drill team. I assured Joe that the Band Boosters Club would give him all of the complete uniforms he needed, and also that they would financially assist him in purchasing other equipment he would need to field a representative drill team worthy of exhibition and competition.

I further assured Joe that, once he informed me that his unit was ready to perform, from that time on, the Douglass Drill Team, "Flight A," would automatically be included in any outdoor activity that included the Eagle Band, thus making the drill team a pertinent part of the marching lineup. They would work in tandem with the band to bring further glory to Frederick Douglass Elementary Junior Senior High School. Joe wanted a few days to make his decision. When he did, Joe, in his usual quiet manner, slowly nodded his head in agreement. We then solemnly shook hands, which sealed the deal.

A call went out for all persons interested in becoming a member of the drill team to meet on a specific day and time. Quite a few students answered the call. Drills were held each evening, along with the band, in a separate area. The final drill team members were selected by Joe.

Oliver Gray, a tall, athletic-type student with a military bearing, was chosen as Drill Team Leader, with the rank of Captain. Soon, the drill team made quite a name for itself performing in parades, competitions, and other school events, such as homecomings, etc. They made quite a striking picture with their white helmets, puttees (a canvas snap covering the lower leg), gloves, and rifles.

Trip to the World's Fair

The crowning achievement of the Douglass Eagle Marching Band and Drill Team occurred during the summer of 1965. It was in April when our principal, Mr. Robert F. Frisby, received a communication from the governor's office, requesting that our stellar marching band and drill team perform at the World's Fair, Maryland Pavilion. Mr. Frisby called me to his office, handed me the letter to read, and asked my feelings on the matter.

For an answer, I let out a loud, "Wow, Mr. Frisby! This is an honor any high school band could hope to achieve!"

Mr. Frisby laughed and said, "Okay, Battle, you have my permission to participate. However, this project entails countless logistical problems, which can only be solved with the help of (and at this junction we both chorused) 'The Band Booster Club'." Mr. Frisby then said, "I'll inform the Board, and you call a special meeting of the Band Boosters as soon as possible."

I immediately went to my office and wrote up an announcement to be read to all students at the dismissal bell. I called for a very special meeting of the Band Boosters Club, and Mr. Ennis, to be held that coming Thursday, two days hence. There was a huge turnout for the meeting. This was the first time that a "called" meeting had been held. The parents filed in, some with apprehensive looks on their faces, all eyes focused on me. Finally, Mr. Robert Pinkney, the Band Boosters Club president, called the meeting to order and, without any fanfare, turned the floor over to me.

"Ladies and gentlemen," I said. "I'd like to read to you a communication that Mr. Frisby received from the governor's office a few days ago." As soon as I finished reading the letter, the band room literally exploded with cheers and applause.

After the commotion died down, I launched into the overall project and sketched for them on the chalkboard some of the problems to be solved and the obstacles facing us. For example: How many chaperones? How many buses and what size overall? What would the cost of the trip be? And so it went. At this juncture, without further direction from me, the parents started listing the necessary committees to be set up. We ended the meeting knowing that the various committees would meet separately to study and research their specific sphere of responsibility, later coming together to report their findings. Time was our biggest enemy, as we had only three months to get our act together.

In the meantime, the marching band and the drill team were doing their share to prepare for an outstanding performance by stepping up their practice schedule. Rehearsals were extended one and one-half hours each day to take advantage of daylight saving time, which doubled our after school practice to three hours.

We were determined to strive for perfection. We trained just as hard as the football team did in spring practice. We went on extended marching drills. The heat took its toll on some members. The drummers raised the decibel level to new highs – new blisters came and went on their hands and fingers. Perspiration flowed freely from all persons involved: The Flag Corps, the Banner Corps, the Color Guard, the Majorettes, the Instrumentalists, and the Douglass Drill Team, Flight A. Altogether, we fielded a full complement of over 150 members. Indeed, this small country school located in the middle of tobacco land was a formidable force with which to be reckoned. Finally, the magical day rolled around. We met at Douglass at two AM on a Saturday in July 1965. The complete entourage filled five buses. Each bus carried seven or eight chaperones. Instruments were loaded in the baggage compartments of each bus. When all band members, drill team members, chaperones, and others were seated, students from the Photography Club climbed aboard and took pictures of each section. We had a photo of every person, where they sat on the bus, as well as his or her signature. I vowed that each person would be accounted for, going and returning. The trip up was very, very quiet. Everybody slept … except me.

We rolled into Flushing Meadows, New York, around seven AM. The buses made excellent time because, at those early hours, there was little traffic to contend with. We slowly made our way to the beautiful and expansive Maryland Pavilion. We were met by a courteous staff, who directed the performers to where they could leave their instruments and freshen up.

Thirty minutes later we were directed to the dining room area set aside for us. Here we were treated to a most lavish meal. Actually, it was more like a brunch, what with omelets, sausages, fresh fruit, rolls, etc. We really "chowed down."

After eating, the bandsmen and drill team members were free to sightsee for one hour. They were divided into groups of 10, each accompanied by two chaperones. The early hours meant that the crowds were small, thus permitting the groups to visit many other pavilions, and not be tied up in long lines. At 11 AM, the groups all drifted in together.

Showtime was at exactly 12 noon. There was an exciting aura to everything. The band members and drill team members changed into their uniforms. The majorettes were scurrying around with their makeup kits; the color guards were double checking their flags and rifles. The whole scene on the surface gave the appearance of utter mayhem. However, to me, it all came under the heading of coordinated independence. At 11:45 AM, the band and the drill team lined up outside the pavilion. There was a very broad area set aside in which we could perform, its dimensions being approximately 50 yards wide and 70 yards long.

As we assembled, the crowds came from all directions and literally surrounded us. The press was everywhere, taking photographs nonstop as we were all at parade rest. The symbol of the 1965 World's Fair, the Unisphere, was in a circle promenade about 50 yards in front of us. It made a most beautiful picture. The stainless steel, three-dimensional globe symbolized the Fair's theme of Peace.

Both drum majors, Silverene Johnson and Carl Windsor, lived up to the tradition of the Douglass drum majors by conducting the Eagle Band as if it were their own. I literally did not have to be there, except to officially take care of the logistics, along with the Band Boosters Club. Actually, both Silverene and Charles were more demanding of the bandsmen than I. They were my extended eyes. Out of the corner of my eye I could see Joe Ennis and his captain, Oliver Gray, of the drill team, in serious pre-show consultation. Behind them, the drill team was lined up, ramrod straight, all eyes focused ahead, helmets gleaming, feet apart at parade rest, rifles at their right toes.

At show time, the two leading drum majors, Silverene and Charles, both whistled all five units of the band to attention. The Banner Bearers, the Color Guard, the Flag Corps, the Majorettes, and the Bandsmen responded as one. Both drum majors executed a sharp about face, raised their batons with a flourish, then snapped off four short blasts on their whistles, and smartly brought their batons down. With an earth-shaking roar, the drummers dug into their parade cadence: snare drums, tenor drums, bass drums, and cymbals all performed in concert. The Drill Team snapped to attention. Both Band and Drill Teams stepped smartly off together.

At the sound of our drums, people started pouring out of the other pavilions and gathered at the parade site. The drum majors signaled for roll-off, then the instrumentalists kicked in with that stirring march, "Them Basses." Douglass put on a great show and the public could not get enough. The bandsmen strutted, holding their instruments high. The majorettes' batons sparkled like diamonds as they were twirled and sent cascading in the air to the embellishment of high precision kicks.

In short, the Douglass Eagle Band and Drill Team truly gave a world-class performance. We were called back for two encores and we really appreciated the spontaneous, extended, heartfelt applause.

After the performance, Mr. Robert Pinkney, president of the Band Boosters Club, and the rest of the chaperones accompanied the weary bandsmen and drill team to their designated area where they packed and secured their instruments, flags, rifles, etc. All of the performers showered and spruced up in the large and plentiful restrooms. Several members changed into sports outfits. Most of the performers, however, elected to stay in their uniforms. I think they truly enjoyed the attention they received from the press and the photographers.

Around three PM, the pavilion's chef came to our area and announced how proud we had made the Maryland staff. Representatives from the governor's office made short speeches and presented several awards to me, the drum majors, and to the Band Boosters President. The awards honored the occasion. The chef then steered us all to the dining room, where we were treated to Maryland crab cakes and other delicious entrees (my favorite was filet mignon). After eating, everyone was free to explore the fairgrounds for one and a half hours.

At six PM, the buses were loaded, heads were counted, and roll was called on each bus. We said a fond goodbye to Flushing Meadows at seven PM. The journey back to Upper Marlboro was very quiet because everybody slept. After literally 12 hours of nonstop activity, we were well spent and ready for the "Land of Nod."

Upon arrival at Douglass, our regular after-parade routine kicked in. All uniforms were hung or draped over chairs, inside out, to permit water evaporation and to avoid mildew affecting the uniforms, as would have happened if the uniforms had been placed in the enclosed closets. As usual, all of the Band Boosters gathered in the band room to report on any urgent problems. The trophy and medallions were secured, and presented to Mr. Frisby, our principal, in September. I thanked the group and Mr. Ennis for their wonderful support, and bade them a safe trip home.

This was actually the second of my two episodes with the New York World's Fairs. The first was in 1939, when I participated in a contest sponsored by Gene Krupa* to find the best drummer in New York City.

He was a small-built man, with thick wavy hair, and was a constant gum chewer—you noticed it when he played. Benny Goodman was the King of Swing; however, Gene Krupa was the heart of his band. The drum solo he took on "Sing, Sing, Sing" is a classic, and drummers still emulate Gene Krupa today. He left Benny Goodman and started his own band. They played the Paramount Theater located near Times Square Manhattan in New York City and were in several Hollywood movies.

The Show Must Go On

In 1975, Al Winfield, leader of the Altones, called to tell me that he had contracted for us to play a gig at Le Fontaine Bleu dance hall in Glen Burnie, Maryland. There are certain places where musicians want to get a gig—Le Fontaine Bleu was one of those very classy halls in which I wanted to play. This club was the piece de resistance of clubs. They had around four regular rooms that were rented out to churches, private clubs, or weddings. Sometimes, all of the rooms were in use at the same time. And on many occasions, the huge screens that separated the rooms were rolled back to disclose one grand ballroom in which many glamorous weddings were held.

* **Author's Note**: *Gene Krupa was the man who lit the fire of imagination among young aspiring drummers of the 1930s and 1940s. There may have been other drummers who had different mind boggling techniques, for example—Max Roach, Buddy Rich, Lionel Hampton, or Chick Webb, to name a few, but none ignited the thrill of drumming like Gene Krupa.*

On this particular night, the rooms were in separate use. If one listened carefully, the boom-boom sounds of bass drums and electric basses could be heard criss-crossing. This was the result of four separate bands playing at the same time in four different places.

All of the bands took their break at the same given time. I followed Al and the others to a large, cavernous kitchen; there I saw two all-Black bands and one mixed-color group. At that time, the Altones were all Colored. We all sat around together and, boy, did we enjoy each other's company. We compared uniforms and exchanged business cards.

The manager came to our area, followed by three employees who carried platters of sandwiches ham, roast beef, and turkey along with a large tub of canned soda of all flavors. The biggest surprise was yet to come. After we had eaten the sandwiches, two employees rolled dessert carts in, each with two shelves holding large flat strawberry shortcakes. The dessert chef came out and, with a large cake spatula, sliced each cake into 4" by 4" squares, then turned around and bade us to help ourselves to small cake-filled platters.

Le Fontaine Bleu really knew how to treat its employees.

Bad Experience in the Backwoods of Virginia

One night the Altones, led by Al Winfield, were packing up because our two-week run was over. Afterwards, we stood around laughing and talking small talk, when a stranger came up to us and said, "Fellows, I've been sitting here all night listening to you. You guys certainly know how to please a crowd."

We looked at him, murmured our thanks, and continued talking about nothing.

He interrupted, held out his hand, and said, "My name is Reet, Reet Pete, and I own a club down in Front Royal, Virginia. We do business in a big way down there; the people come from miles around on Saturdays. We average around 300 or 400 each Saturday and Sunday night."

Al stopped talking, looked at Reet Pete, and said, "So?" and we all laughed.

Pete smiled and said, "I'm offering you a job for next Saturday and Sunday. Tell me, how do you all travel from gig to gig?"

"We load up in two cars," I replied. And I further asked, "Just how much are you offering for playing, both days and travel?"

Pete looked me directly in the eye and said, "Tell you what I'm gonna do, I'll give you each 300 dollars a night for six pieces, plus an extra 100 dollars each for the drivers. How does that sound?"

Al said, "That makes it 38 hundred; put in another 200 for leader's fee and you might have yourself a deal."

Pete said, "You said might, big fellow, why might?"

Al said, "Talk is cheap."

Reet Pete smiled, reached inside his chest pocket, and pulled out a folded paper—a contract. Pete took out a pen, filled in the appropriate blanks with dollar figures, signed his name, and pushed the contract to Al.

Al picked up the contract, read it briefly, then passed it around for each of us to see. Then Al said, "How say you band?" We nodded our heads in agreement, and then Al took the pen and affixed his signature. This was how the average run-of-the-mill business regarding entertainers was conducted. There were no agents or slick, shiny offices. That was for the stars.

That next week, for the most part, the Altones were locked in, planning for their upcoming Saturday and Sunday gig at the "Bar and Grill" in Front Royal, Virginia. We got sectional maps of the area, and roughly plotted how many miles to get there. I could see that we had to navigate over some mountainous areas; the place looked lonesome and forlorn to me on the map. We asked around other musicians to see whether any of them had ever played this joint. To our dismay, none had.

Finally Saturday morning arrived. We loaded into two cars; Al drove one and Buddy, our bassist, drove the other. The trip was smooth and interesting all the way, except for one hair-raising episode coming down a very high mountainside. As we were descending, I noticed that Al had to literally ride his brakes to keep the car under control. I then looked out the rear window to see this large 18-wheeler coming fast. There wasn't anywhere we could pull over; there were trees and rocks covering both sides of the road. Al had a very concerned look on his face as the truck crept closer.

He said, "Grab the seats guys, I've got to speed up to stay ahead of that crazy nut tailgating us."

I noticed the speedometer needle hitting 65, then 70, then 80 miles per hour. The worst part was that this was not exactly a straight road, and I thought I saw a mean grin on the truck driver's face. He knew nothing would happen to him if we crashed.

The speedometer was inching toward 85 when, thank the good Lord, we hurtled pass a road sign that I could barely read due to our speed. "Al," I shouted, "Road rest stop area ahead. Be prepared to veer right!"

Al nodded and just then we saw a single two-car track road veering slightly to our right. Al pointed the car in that direction and dug a new path as small rocks bounced off our sides and windshield. In a nanosecond, we saw the open rest area with parked cars on both sides of the road. Meanwhile Al was riding the brakes, so I reached over and turned the ignition off (to prevent a fire). Al then turned the car up a very slight incline, and we were encased in a heavy cloud of dust as the car rolled to a stop.

Several people ran over to the driver's side to ask, was there a problem? Al took a big breath, looked at the people, laughed and said, "No problem now, but I was trying to get away from that big gorilla chasing me."

Someone in the crowd said, "Man, I know what you mean! It seems that truckers hate passenger cars on this stretch because they say we slow them down and keep them from getting bonuses for rapid delivery."

The rest of the gig panned out fine—we were a hit, Reet Pete was happy, and the money flowed (luckily, not our blood).

Sadness at Pirates Cove

It was in the mid-1980s when we were fortunate enough to be chosen by the manager of Pirates Cove to be the steady entertainment for the supper club. Pirates Cove was located in the in the quiet, sleepy waterfront town of Galesville, Maryland. This club-restaurant was located on the South River. In addition to the evening service, the breakfast crowd on Sunday mornings was always a sellout. There was always a stream of motorboats or launches tying up at Pirates Cove Wharf.

One Saturday morning, Al Winfield, the leader of the Altones, called to tell me that his mother had passed. I expressed my sorrow at this news because I knew what a close relationship Al and his mother enjoyed. Then I said that we have to get a substitute for him because we had to play that evening. Al would have none of that: "I've just got to play, Boots; Mom would want me to carry on!"

I agreed; it would have been very difficult to get a substitute for Al. Al was a first-class entertainer. He played a truly soulful tenor sax and he was a crooner in the Frank Sinatra style.

That evening, after the patrons were completing their supper and preparing to dance, Al took the microphone. Al told the crowd about his mother passing and, in a way that did not offend people who came out for a joyous evening of dining and dancing, he asked that all would dance to the next tune. This was a tribute to her, as she loved to dance. None of us in the band knew what Al was going to play. He took a deep breath and a low wail came from the bell of his horn. The band joined in and, in a moment's time, tears were streaming from Al's eyes as he purred, "Just a Closer Walk with Thee."

Flooding

There were two prestigious supper clubs that kept lists, which musicians tried to get on in order to be "called" by the maitre d' to come and perform. One was the "Pirates Cove" and the other was "Capone's Hideaway." There was no use thinking about Topside; they had had the same group for ages. This club was located at the end of a long country road (actually a main street in the sleepy town of Galesville, Maryland). Galesville is situated right on the waters of South River. It was in a tiny out-of-the-way place; however, it was loaded with activity.

At the dead end of the town road was a very famous inn called the Topside, which featured fish, cuisine, and dancing. The "Topside" featured live Dixieland bands every weekend and always carried a standing room only crowd. If you drove straight ahead, you could run through a narrow stretch of green fields and trees, and run smack into a river. If you turned right on the narrow road, after 50 yards you would see a restaurant called "Steamboat Landing." Steamboat had a dock that went about 25 yards out into the water. That is where the boat traffic docked and entered the club. Usually they were in swim gear, but covered with white terrycloth robes. Steamboat was noted for its seafood and excellent roast beef.

If you turned left at Topside, you would travel about 25 yards to a small wooden trellis fence opening. When you went through the gate, a large shipyard would greet you. There you would see several small yachts in various states of repair. On the left side of this shipyard was a very famous dinner-dancing supper club, Pirates Cove, also located right on the water. This was the pearl of supper clubs. They had a very active docking wharf where customers jumped right from their crafts to the part of the restaurant that catered to the wet crowd.

As you drove by Pirates Cove, you went up a slight incline past a property line of fences and trees into another large square. Sitting on the edge of the water with an outside seating deck with benches and tables (each holding very large colorful shade umbrellas), the entrance to the club was at ground level, surrounded by huge panes of dark glass. This was called "Capone's Hideaway." This supper club also catered to the motorboat trade. There were several private dining rooms in one area and a place for the band at the end of this room. These clubs, particularly on Sundays, were so crowded; there were always lines waiting.

The Topside and Pirates Cove closed early … around midnight. However, that was just the beginning of action in dear ol' Galesville.

It made for a most beautiful setting, what with the gentle surf lapping at the shore rocks, just out of reach of the sloping ground leading to the tables. At one corner of the outside area was our band, the Altones. When we opened up and played, you could hear us all around the shore. We would start playing at twilight and the combination of yachts, motorboats, beautiful scantily clad ladies, and those patrons who came in white tuxedos and summer evening dresses, created a most delightful ambiance for our music. Then, around one AM, there was a surge of musicians and regular guests who proceeded to jam pack all of the available tables. The area became as active as a beeline … liquor and food filled all trays carried by the young waiters and waitresses.

The guest musicians who came in from the closed Topsides and Pirates Cove took the stage and blended with the house band (us) to perform heavenly music. There was truly dancing and romancing under a starry canopy.

As time went by and the fame of the Altones grew, we found ourselves courted by the owners of Pirates Cove and finally got a steady gig there. I recall one St. Valentines Day evening, the club was closed to the general public. A couple rented out Pirates Cove for the night to put on a very lavish wedding.

There was nothing for want that night. Guests were plied with gift bags containing wedding mementos to honor the bride and groom. Each bag contained such wonderful gifts as ladies' watches with silver bands, unique cigarette lighters, fancy gold key chains, and vials of expensive perfume.

Well, about midnight, clouds rolled in to cover the twinkling stars, but water taxis kept stopping at Pirates Cove wharf and unloading wedding guests. Soon, around 12:30 AM, hard drops of rain started to pelt everybody. Shortly thereafter, a steady, heavy downpour ensued and the manager directed the band to set up inside, and invited the guests immediately to come inside to await food and drink.

We moved inside and picked up where we left off; the music was groovy and everybody was doing great. Around one AM, I noticed the outside area deck was covered with water. Soon water flowed inside from under all the doors. It wasn't long before the water was lapping at my drum set. I took my feet off my drum and cymbal pedals only to feel them splash in standing water. I called the manager and told him that the band had to pack up. The father of the young lady urged the band to continue because more people had not yet arrived. I pointed to the water and told him it was too dangerous to attempt to perform because the electric guitar, electric bass, and public address system could electrocute us. At this point, the manager said, "Let's move upstairs and set up."

A few minutes later, all of us went upstairs. I had to make several trips to get all of my drums, bass, snare, bells, cymbals, and cases.

The patrons were laughing and joking when the lights went out and all electricity failed. Undaunted, the manager and restaurant help started lighting candles of all colors; as it turned out, things got real romantic. The music was very soft with the bass and guitar playing acoustically, and I used brushes instead of sticks. The water stopped rising after it spread to the steps. We played for an hour more before the celebrated couple said, "Goodnight."

The band packed up their instruments, and gingerly maneuvered through the ankle-high water to their cars.

A Learning Experience at Gallaudet University

Several years ago, Al Winfield, leader of the band in which I played, The Altones, called and told me that we had a gig at Gallaudet University. I was very excited because college gigs are usually good for musicians—we get fed, and the music the students like is fun to play. I had never played for an audience that included people with a combination of hearing, speaking, and sight impairment.

As we were setting up our instruments, a crowd of students was signing to each other as they pointed out different sounds. When we started tuning up, a pleasant glow came over their faces as each musician tuned his horn. However, broad smiles and laughter resulted when I went through the process of tuning and adjusting my snares, tom-toms, and bass drums (I think the various vibrations of each type of drum had this effect on them).

At eight PM, the President of Gallaudet came to the bandstand and requested a loud roll and cymbal crash before he welcomed everybody. Usually when we play for a dinner or dance, there is a lot of commotion and conversation that can be heard before we start our first number. Tonight, however, there was an eerie silence accompanied by a plethora of hand movements of people "loudly" signing each other.

At 8:15 PM sharp, Al "stomped off" the tempo for "When You're Smiling." In a few seconds, the floor was filled with couples. Before the lights dimmed, I noticed that many couples were holding balloons, and all were dancing to the beat.

After the first tune, I called one of the instructors over and asked him about the balloons. He explained to me that the students could feel the beat through the balloon. Also, the ballroom floor was made of a very special durable, but porous, wood that reverberates through to the shoe soles.

During our break, a few instructors came to our table with a very beautiful, charming young lady. They introduced her all around and requested that she sing when we got back to the bandstand. They said that she used to sing; however, she was involved in a terrible accident that resulted in the loss of her hearing.

After the break, this young lady came to the bandstand and requested a very complicated song to sing. The title was Duke Ellington's "Sophisticated Lady." Boy, we had to scramble to get the charts so that we could accompany her. She sounded like a real pro, and we did our best to keep up with her. I often wonder what became of her, just what did the future hold for her? She and her fellow students were really not handicapped, but they had special needs: a balloon to feel the beat, or a floor that sent reverberations through the soles of their shoes.

Dressed to a "T"

Al Winfield, the leader of the Altones, passed away in 1985. This was a great blow to the band—we had dates to play and there was the problem of someone to step up and be the new leader. The remaining members of the group at that time were: Jack King (bass), Al Carter (guitar), and myself, Boots Battle (drums). We had a meeting one night to discuss upcoming gigs and to find someone to replace Al (tenor sax and vocals).

At the very start of the meeting, Al Carter said, "I vote that we select Boots to be the leader. He has had more experience than any of us in leading. Besides, Boots has a lot of contacts for possible gigs in Anne Arundel County."

I accepted on one condition. "We must wear tuxedos for every gig, black in the winter and white coats in the summer." I got the idea of wearing tuxedos years ago when I was watching a boxing show on television. At the end of the show, the announcer interviewed a popular boxer named Henry Armstrong. At one point, the announcer said to Henry Armstrong, "Henry, I notice you always wear tuxedos when you are a guest on television. Why is that?"

Henry Armstrong smiled and said, "Perhaps a million people are inviting me into their homes. The greatest respect I can show is to look my best."

The Altones adhered to this tradition for many, many years: black tuxedos in the winter, white coats in the summer, or white formal guayabera shirts on those steaming "dog days" of August.

One day in June, this policy proved to be a big problem. I got a call from the manager of Tom's Crab House, located on South River in Deale, Maryland. Tom's was a very popular eatery—they had large ads in the local newspapers and eating at Tom's was the talk of the town. Wearing white coats, black bowties, and cummerbunds, we arrived at Tom's. The first thing I noticed was that, in place of the usual round tables set up for formal dinners, there were rows of benches with little metal hammers and things that looked like small ice picks at each setting.

After we were set up and had tested the public address system, people started literally running in, dressed in swimsuits, halters, sport short-sleeve shirts, etc. Well the main point was, there wasn't any dancing. People were engrossed in cracking crabs and to me, the band was way overdressed. That was the one and only time that I felt out of place in a tuxedo and I never accepted another gig there.

Tragedy

One of the most desired gigs by all musicians in Annapolis was to be in the band that played at Jason's. Now the owner of Jason's was a big-time supplier in the beverage business. He opened up this beautiful supper-dancing club at one of the busiest intersections in

Annapolis (it was just a walk across a little bridge to the famous "Annapolis Yacht Club").

Upon the death of Al Winfield in 1985, I became head of the Altones. Swing was our thing, and we were in demand by all of the high society organizations. As luck would have it, we were contracted to play at Jason's for one year. We were scheduled for Friday nights and Sunday nights (Jason had different groups playing all the other nights). We had a smooth-playing group, consisting of Dennis 'Tank' Davis (tenor sax), Al "Hot Poppa" Carter (guitar), Jack King (bass), Roy "Boots" Battle (drums), and Artie Dicks on vocals (Artie was a former member of the Ink Spots). The other groups at Jason's would play that loud "punk" music and drew a young crowd. However, on Friday and Sunday nights, the older "smoothies" would be our patrons. Music of the 1920s, 1930s, and 1940s was the order of the day. We had the roving microphone (cordless) set up and Artie Dicks would move from table to table, singling out beautiful females and making them feel that he was just singing to them. When he sang, "I Only Have Eyes for You" or "You're Just Too Marvelous," he would take the lady's hand and literally lead them through paradise.

On a hot night in August, we were playing a foot-stomping, hip-rocking strong, but soft back beat of a gut-bucket blues when I noticed a crowd gathering in front of the bandstand. Usually when this occurs, a couple is showing off with special steps. Somehow, this was different. I noticed a lady running out the front door yelling something. Then Mr. Fleet, the club owner, came to me and asked me to stop the music. He then went to the microphone and asked everybody to go to their tables and let the person on the floor get air. A few seconds later, I saw flashing red and white lights through the club windows. Then I saw two paramedics enter the club, carrying a stretcher. They stopped in front of the band, leaned over the fallen patron, gave him CPR, then they rolled him onto the stretcher and exited the club.

We finished the night, but our hearts were not in the music of joy we projected. "Laugh, Clown, Laugh" forced its way into my thoughts. Later that night, it was announced that the patron had passed away—he literally danced himself to death! I contacted the family, the Altones sent flowers, and I attended the funeral.

Hyatt Regency

Usually, a band is hired on the socialite circuit due to "word of mouth." One day, this very distinguished gentleman, dressed in the formal dark blues of the Army, came up to me during a break when we were playing for a wedding. (I noticed he had a gold star on each shoulder.) He tapped me on the shoulder and stated, "May I have a word with you, Mr. Battle?"

I turned and motioned him to the terrace where there was relative quiet. He began by pulling out his wallet and showing me a photo of five beautiful females. "These are my daughters," he said. "Now here's the plan. I want to engage you now to play the music for each daughter's wedding. I know this will cover a span of five or six years."

Well, I never was involved in a proposition such as this before. However, I did hear of society orchestras, such as Eddie Duchin, being contracted to play for soon-to-be-debutantes who were just 12 or 13. As it were, all of the General's daughters were present, so the General showed me to his table, where he introduced me to his wife, his daughters, and their escorts.

After the General explained why I was at his table, I turned to his youngest daughter and said, "You could be making a big mistake. You might not like the brand of music we'll be playing when you're ready to say 'I do'."

She laughed and said, "Just keep swinging, Sir." Then she twirled around and was lost in the crowd.

As each joyful event was scheduled, we fulfilled our contract to the last happy bride.

Nordstrom's

One night, the Altones got a special gig, playing for the perfume and Women's Department, given by the female employees of Nordstrom Department Store. Now Nordstrom's was the elite big name store located in the Annapolis mall. The evening was a fashion show, topped off with a special time when all the patrons could go into another room and purchase special silver and gold jewelry at outstanding discounts. Meanwhile, the people were enthralled with the soft, swinging sounds of the Altones, and the sexy, sultry vocals of our singer, Marilyn Carlson. We were all a big hit. When each number ended, we were greeted with hearty applause.

One of the salespeople present was a longtime friend of my wife. Page Garrett Smith worked at the perfume counter of Nordstrom's and she fit right in with the entire ambiance there. Page was a very attractive tall, classy lady with swept-back hair and a soft café-au-lait complexion. During the break, she said to me, "Battle, I was just talking with one of the managers at Nordstrom's. He said that he loved your music and enjoyed listening to you play. I told him that he should consider getting the Altones to play in the store on Saturday afternoons."

The next month, I received a call from a lady who was in charge of community relations at Nordstrom's, and she asked me to have lunch with her the next day. So I put on my "Sunday best" and, at the agreed upon time, I entered Nordstrom's. There was a musician playing old favorites on the piano. I strolled to Page's counter and we talked for a few minutes about the gig a few weeks before. Then I asked her where I should go to meet the coordinator, and she picked up the microphone and paged her. In a few seconds, the coordinator was in front of me, extending a very welcome hand. I followed her down a hall lined with photos of early Nordstrom days. Another female employee greeted us and showed us to a small room with a large round table filled with sliced ham, turkey, cheese, rolls, Swiss meatballs, and trays of condiments.

We both took seats, made small talk about our last gig, and then she said, "Mr. Battle."

I interrupted her right away and said, "Please call me Boots."

She smiled and said, "Boots, how would you feel about signing a six-month contract to have the Altones play here in center store from two to six PM each Saturday? You would play for two hours, with a lunch break for half an hour, then play again until six PM." She continued, "Just instrumentalists, no vocals, because that would interfere with our announcements. The pay will be 500 dollars; you divide it as you wish."

The gig was ideal. It did not interfere with our Saturday night gigs and, surprise, we got many wedding gigs as a result. It was so satisfying to see the delight of the patrons as they found relaxation and rejuvenation in our soothing sounds.

Happy Harbor Inn

Shady Side, Maryland, is a very popular place, especially in the summertime. You see, there are countless night clubs and eateries located right on the South River. The clubs have wharves where leisure boats can sail right up and dock. The owners then go up to the outside bars to sit down at tables equipped with huge shade umbrellas. The patrons are serviced by cheerful waitresses who bring liquid libations or meals, usually of seafood.

One Saturday afternoon, as I was leaving a grocery store down in Shady Side, a pleasant-looking blonde lady said, "Hold up, Mr. Battle, I'd like a few words with you."

Well, I stopped and looked the young lady in the eye. She looked familiar but, at the moment, I couldn't place exactly who she was.

"If you're not engaged tomorrow, I'd like to hire your combo to play Sunday afternoon for a few hours at my place, The Happy Harbor Inn."

Then it hit me; this was Karen Sturgell, sister of Robert Sturgell. Hastily, I rolled over the facts and information in my mind as Karen was talking. Robert Sturgell attended Southern High School where my daughter Lisa went. Both Robert and Lisa were wonderful students at school and became good friends. I recalled going to Robert's house to purchase some very good jumbo shrimp from Robert's father, who was a big-time east coast salesman. I also quickly remembered that Robert went on to the United States Naval Academy, made a great service record for himself and, later, turned politician. He ran for a position with the state administration. I remember voting for him because he had the same fine liberal ideas that I felt could have benefited Anne Arundel county.

Through my thoughts, I could see Karen's lips moving and I heard myself saying, "The terms are fine. I'll supply a three-piece combo for the agreed-upon price for four hours starting at two PM tomorrow, Sunday." I went straight home and called Bob Price, a great keyboard player and singer, and Dennis 'Tank' Davis, tenor sax extraordinaire.

Now that evening, I started having second thoughts about playing there because the Happy Harbor was frequented by two rival motorcycle gangs. I really was not certain that my brand of music was the motorcycle club's cup of tea.

Well, Sunday rolled around and the Altones met at the Happy Harbor. It was a beautiful sunny day in August, and we set up on the outdoor bandstand. This was very unique because the bandstand was built on an extension that ran right out over the water. I had to be very, very careful setting up my drums to see that no part rolled because of the danger of falling into the river. The river was at least four feet deep around us.

Our dress was very informal; I wore black lightweight trousers, a white short-sleeve sport shirt, and a very lightweight golf jacket because it did get a bit breezy on the water. The back of my jacket was emblazoned with large black letters around a P-51 fighter plain; the letters said, "Tuskegee Airman."

In no time, after we were set up and ready to play, the waitress at the dock bar came over with bacon, lettuce, and tomato sandwiches, plus a large pitcher full of iced tea. She said there were plenty of refills for us, to just call her. We also set up a cardboard "Kitty" on the floor in front of the band with a sign around its neck saying "Please feed the kitty."

Soon, the tables were literally filled up; there were no more stools open at the dock bar. The deck was very crowded and noisy when I stomped off the first selection. It was a swinging vocal rendition of "Come on Home Bill Bailey." The deck was filled with rough-looking motorcycle riders and beautiful ladies dressed in pants and gang jackets along with heavy boots. Heavily bearded and mustached guys came up to me and shouted over my cymbal playing, "Do y'all know 'Rocky Top Tennessee', 'Beer Barrel Polka,' 'Tennessee Waltz,' or the like?"

Well we played each and every request. Bob Price, on our electric piano, crooned and Dennis "Tank" Davis played soulful riffs.

At break time, I took our empty pitcher over to the dock bar for a refill. While I was waiting, my back was facing the dance floor. Someone came up to me, pulled me gently around and here, looking at me in the eyes, was a lean good-looking, battle-scarred face. He wore a red bandana around his forehead and heavy chains secured his wallet to his side pocket. He looked at me and said, "Sir, I want to thank you personally for what you and those other Black fliers did for our country. You had to go through hell, I know, but here's my hand." Then he turned to the dock waitress and said for all to hear, "Give this gentleman anything he wants to drink or eat. I, Alibi, will pay for same."

Annapolis Yacht Club

I truly think the defining point of my band, the Altones, came in the 1980s when we gained "House Band" status at the Annapolis Yacht

Club (AYC). The AYC was located in Annapolis Harbor. Needless to say, it was the berth of small sailing boats, houseboats, and large and small motor launches. The clubhouse was a three-story building, which was a beehive of activity, especially on weekends.

It all happened one night when we were playing a private party for Mr. Johnson (the owner of the very prestigious Johnson's haberdashery located on State Circle, Annapolis). Mr. John Boswell, manager of the Annapolis Yacht Club, approached me during the band's break, introduced himself, and said to me, "Mr. Battle, I'm interested in hiring your combo to be our house band upstairs in the main ballroom. Would you be interested in a long-term contract?"

I replied, "Mr. Boswell, that sounds swell. However, everything depends upon the details; you can understand that."

He said, "Perfectly. Why don't you drop by tomorrow, we'll talk about the gig, and I'll answer all your questions."

The next day, Sunday, I went to the AYC and there was a real flurry of movement that greeted me as I entered the side door. Waiters and waitresses were buzzing around with trays of delicious-looking food. One chef dressed in his chef's hat, white coat, and hounds tooth trousers asked if he could help me. I informed him that I had an appointment with Mr. Boswell. He pointed to an elevator and directed me to Mr. Boswell's office on the second floor level.

Mr. Boswell beckoned me in through the open glass doors. Rising as I entered, he motioned me to a seat in front of a huge desk. He then asked if I would like anything to drink.

"Coffee," I replied. "Lots of sugar and cream." (I hate coffee with just plain milk.)

He leaned over a box, pushed a button, and put in an order for two coffees. In a few minutes, a waiter appeared, carrying a tray with a small silver coffee pot with accessories, including a small assortment of pastries. Mr. Boswell told me how much he enjoyed my band. He said we played the type of music he knew the patrons would enjoy listening and dancing to. I then asked him about the hours and pay.

Mr. Boswell replied that the contract would be for six months with provisions of extension. We would play each Saturday night from seven PM until 11 PM for the amount of 500 each night. I agreed to the terms, and signed the contract, which stated we would start the coming Saturday.

"I like the way your group dresses," he said. "The tuxedoes add a good touch to our ambiance."

Opening night for us was like a page out of *Glamour*. The lights were low and ladies seemed to sparkle all over. The men I noticed all seemed to wear the yachting captain's attire: a navy blue sport coat, white shirt, black bowtie, khaki dress trousers, and black patent leather shoes. It surprised me to see so many young blondes coupled with elderly gentlemen.

A bonus of the gig was that we were hired to play some Sunday afternoon affairs at the yacht club; we also got paid extra when we played for special occasions, such as "The Blessing of the Fleet."

27th Tuskegee National Convention

Washington, DC

In August 1998, the Tuskegee Airmen, Incorporated, held its 27th national convention in Washington, DC. This event is the most important activity of the year for Tuskegee Airmen because each chapter and individual therein are affected by the decisions voted upon by the elected body. At that time, there were 41 active chapters throughout the United States. The convention was officially in session from August 4th through August 9th.

I'm an original Tuskegee Airman and my chapter, the east coast chapter, is located in Washington, DC. We were responsible for hosting the convention at the J.W. Marriott Hotel. Mrs. Cora M. "Tess"

Spooner, wife of then Brigadier General Richard Spooner, was co-chair person, along with now-deceased Alonzo Smith, Jr. I'm compelled at this time to extend a hearty thanks to Joy Branham and Jim Pryde who, thankfully, are there to answer all my inquiries and to fill in the potholes on my bumpy highway of knowledge.

It was my burning desire to have my band, the Altones, play for the opening welcome reception to be held on August 4th in the Grand Ballroom from seven PM until 10 PM. I called "Tess" and expressed my desire to play for the opening session. "Tess" said that she would take this before the committee.

One week later, "Tess" called me and said, "Boots, I took your proposal to the committee and they said that 500 dollars was too much and that the funds were stretched too far." Then she added, with a twinkle in her voice, "Boots, the contract is in the mail. I said, to heck, we should have some classy music to greet the Tuskegee Airmen and their guests."

My heart went out to "Tess." You couldn't help but love her because, if "Tess" believed in anything, she'd just let the dice roll and the devil may care.

There were over 500 guests with standing room only to greet the Altones. Later that night, I asked our suave, velvet tone crooner Artie Dicks to dedicate "I Only Have Eyes for You" to "Tess."

Tribute to Clemmie Weems

Clemmie Weems was one of my first outstanding woodwind instrumentalists. Clemmie was in the 1953 class and he excelled on the B-flat clarinet. The basic tenet of being a Douglass Band member was: "Practice, Practice, Practice." I'll never forget that thrill I received when one Saturday morning, our band was invited to attend a clinic given by the Navy School of Music, which was headquartered in Anacostia, DC.

Clemmie's father, Gary Weems, decided to drive. We would meet the band at nine AM at the entrance to the Navy School of Music. Mr. Weems picked me up and then took me to his house. From there he would transport Clemmie, plus three other bandsmen and myself. When Mr. Weems parked, he asked me to come in and meet his lovely wife, Suzy. As we entered the family room we were greeted by Mrs. Weems with hot coffee and doughnuts.

However, what really caught my attention was the sound of a piano in an adjoining room. I then recognized what was being played—it was the overture to "The Student Prince." I looked around questioningly, and Mrs. Weems said, "Go on in, Mr. Battle; I'm sure you will know who's playing."

With that, I immediately turned and entered the room. My mouth flew open, because seated at the piano was my star pupil, Clemmie Weems. On his own, he had picked out the melody and chords of the selection our band was rehearsing. This alone told me why he stood so tall in his studies.

Clemmie graduated from Douglass Elementary Junior Senior High School and won a music scholarship to Howard University. Following his graduation from Howard University, he did a stint in the United States Army. As one can imagine, he became an integral participant in the Army Band.

Tribute to Isaac Cook

I would like to take this opportunity to acknowledge truly one of the greatest Band Directors to ever share his big talent in Prince George's County, where he taught at Fairmont Heights Senior High School. I'm speaking of "Sir" Isaac Cook (as we lovingly called him). "Ike" came upon the scene as the second Black band director in Prince George's County (myself being the first).

Ike was a great brass man and he turned out some stellar trumpet players, such as Lawrence Jackson, Jr., who once was one of the coveted United States Army Band's Herald Trumpet players (Lawrence Jackson, Sr., was principal of Douglass High School where I taught for 16 years).

In addition, Ike turned out some wonderful woodwind players. In particular, I'm speaking of G. James Gholson who, through his expertise, held a seat in the United States Navy Band. Ike had the respect of all the Band Directors, Black or White. We truly regret his passing away at the beginning of the millennium.

Tribute to Max Roach (1924-2007)

The World's Best Drummer and My Friend

Max and I both grew up in the Bedford-Stuyvesant section of Brooklyn, New York. We were both around the same age (14) when we found the object that forged our friendship—drums. Max made a name for himself with his wonderful improvisations with rhythms when he sat in with various bands. On the other hand, I was known for the driving beat I gave to groups.

Around this time, the late 1930s, swing was the type of music demanded by soloists and by dancers. They would find their niche with the solid four-four time to groove by.

With an opposite view were the Nuevo musicians who embellished on the standard time beats and established offbeat, intricate passages on chord structure. That challenged conventional playing.

Max Roach belonged to the above group. IIe always said, "The drum should be played like a melody." Max played for a very popular band in Brooklyn when we were growing up. This was a group known as the Clarence Beery Orchestra. Every Sunday night, they would perform at the Seagull Beach, not too far from Coney Island.

The band turned out some excellent sidemen, such as Sonny Payne on baritone horn, and Leonard Gaskins on acoustic bass, in addition to Max Roach.

There was a very popular dance spot in Brooklyn called the "Putnam Central" (it was located on Putnam Avenue). Actually, it was an old brownstone house renovated into a small dance floor and bandstand. There was a small bar in the back and there were tables lining the walls. One day at noon, I received a call from Max. He said, "Boots, I'm at the Central Inn; come on over and we'll do some drum duets from the drum book."

Max and I always got along out of great respect for each other's talent. However, the real bonding and binding of our friendship came about because we both could read the charts. Sight reading was our challenge to each other. Max would get a new selection, put it on the music stand, and say, "Your move!"

One day, I tried to trick him. I got a first clarinet chart to one of Mozart's classical pieces. I told Max to close his eyes and not to open them until I tapped on my drum. Well, when I tapped, Max opened his eyes, then looked at me and broke out in his hearty laugh. "Stand back rookie," he said to me and, with a flourish of his sticks, proceeded to rip through the chart in no time. I just shook my head; so much for trickery!

In 1983, my son LeRoy, Junior, was in his third year as a music major and a junior at Howard University in Washington, DC. At the time, I was playing a gig up in Brooklyn, New York. Well, Le Roy and a few of his classmates (music majors) heard that Max Roach was over in Crampton Hall setting up his drums for a concert that he and his choir were going to give later that evening. LeRoy and his friends went over, but they couldn't see so well from where they stood, so they, en masse, went up on the stage. Max's back was to them, as he was bent over tuning his snare drum. When he finished, he straightened up and turned around. He took one look at the students, and literally yelled out, "Boots Battle!" My son was so proud, he telephoned me that night.

Band Members Give Tribute to LeRoy A. Battle

Once a Douglass Bandsman, Always a Douglass Bandsman

Becoming a member of the Douglass Band was my goal from the moment I entered Frederick Douglass High School. Band members were part of an elite group within the school community under the direction of our revered Mr. Battle. To be a part of an organization that was supported by the students, the faculty, the parents, and the community gave us an awesome feeling of pride. I enjoyed four years with the band as a clarinet player and as a majorette. To this day, I proudly tell the world of the marvelous accomplishments of the Douglass Band. All of this was made possible by a skilled musician, great motivator, and just a wonderful, caring individual we lovingly call Mr. Battle.

—Former Douglass High School Member
Elizabeth Gwendolyn "Susie" Proctor

What It Meant to Me to Be in the Douglass High School Band

I believe I was in the eighth grade when Mr. LeRoy Battle approached me about becoming a Douglass Band member. At first, I was somewhat reluctant because some of my schoolmates had told me that Mr. Battle could really be a "tough" guy. However, "Joe" Gordon, who at the time played the baritone horn, convinced me to give it a try.

Mr. Battle thought I should start with the sousaphone, the biggest, most awkward horn in the band. Man, that thing was so heavy; the

Lord had to help me when the wind started to blow during parades. I would take two steps forward, three sideways, and about five backwards, then smile. Mr. Battle used to say, "Newman, why can't you walk straight?"

I wanted to say, "You carry this big damned horn and see how straight you walk!" But it was fun!

However, from the time I picked up that sousaphone, there was no looking or turning back. A whole new world opened up to me, filled with endless possibilities, not just with music. I began to appreciate other areas of my life, and my relations with others improved as I reached out more. I learned the value of carrying my own fair share of the workload to improve individual and organizational performance.

Also, during my senior year in high school, Mr. Battle and Mrs. Hazel Rich told me that I could be the first Newman to go to college, and I could get a scholarship. Mr. Battle, in particular, urged me to attend college. He was very persistent. Mr. Battle even gave me the chance to use the scholarship to attend the University of Maryland, College Park, and become the first Black to be in that band and orchestra.

However, I did not feel up to blazing that trail and chose to attend the University of Maryland, Eastern Shore. I went off to Maryland State College and earned my Bachelor's Degree, while playing baseball up and down the East Coast.

After college, I served two years in the United States Peace Corps as a teacher in East Africa in Blantyre, Malawi. I had many fun days there playing my trumpet in the villages, while the Africans danced and played drums.

After the Peace Corps, I was inducted into the United States Army and spent two years in Frankfurt, Germany, later earning my Master's Degree from Columbia University. I now work for the United States Department of Education, and lead a pretty darn good life.

I owe all of this primarily to Mr. Battle because he was the one teacher who inspired and motivated all of us to be the very best we could be. Mr. Battle not only said the right words, but he modeled the behavior he expected of us. He certainly "walked his talk" and not just when he felt like it. He did it, day in and day out. Under Mr. Battle's leadership, the band grew and blossomed into one of the best (if not the best) in the state of Maryland.

As a result of Mr. Battle's teaching, training, and leadership, I was fortunate enough to be selected to the Maryland All-State Band during my senior year. If I recall correctly, there were only three Blacks selected, and two of those were from Mr. Battle's band. I was very proud, and felt very comfortable playing music in the All-State Band with almost all White kids because Mr. Battle had taught me well. I knew my music, and I was proud to show my "stuff" and represent the Douglass High School Band.

As a Douglass Band member, I developed pride, self-confidence, self-reliance, and learned the importance of teamwork, as well as the values of being persistent and resourceful. I was not only lucky to have had Mr. Battle as teacher and coach, but also as a friend.

Thanks so much for being there for me, as well as for countless others. You are "The Man!"

— Former Douglass High School Band Member
Lawrence Newman

PART IV

ACCOLADES, AWARDS, SPEECHES, VISITS

My Visit to the Federal Bureau of Investigation (F.B.I.)

My first visit to the F.B.I. In Washington, DC, was on Friday, September 29, 2000. The F.B.I. employees set that day as the date to honor the Tuskegee Airmen. There were five of us from the Tuskegee Airmen's Speakers' Bureau who attended: George "Hank" Henry (our supervisor), J. T. Valentine, Samuel Rhodes, Leo R. Gray, and myself. The F.B.I. building itself is an architect's noble dream. It is huge and impressive. We were ushered to our seats, which faced an overwhelming crowd of 300 or more employees. We were welcomed with a talk given by Thomas J. Pickard, the Deputy Director of the F.B.I., followed by a warm introduction rendered by Section Chief Dennis R. Weaver. Each Tuskegee Airman took the microphone and related a special experience he had as a cadet or officer. "Hank" previously had piqued the audience's interest by detailing the start of the "Tuskegee Experience." The philosophy of some powers-that-be was: "Black men were too ignorant to master the technique of flying." The Tuskegee Airmen, of course, put that malicious belief to an end.

For me, personally, this visit to the F.B.I. was the most wonderful, warm treatment I had received in my first five years as a member of the Speakers' Bureau of the East Coast Chapter of the Tuskegee Airmen. The key word that describes this visit was, I think, respect. No matter where my eyes wandered, they were met with a slight nod and smile in my direction. Hundreds of pictures were taken. It seemed that everybody wanted to pose with the Tuskegee Airmen. Also, we had to autograph well over 100 items. Someone was assigned to our table to bring us food and drink. The menu included: fried chicken, meatballs, pasta, salads, rolls, cakes, pies, grape punch, and more. The food was fabulous and plentiful.

After the affair, we headed towards our rides. However, my arthritic leg was acting up and Section Chief Dennis R. Weaver, without hesitation, held my left elbow as we inched the 100 yards to the van. He lifted my leg to help me negotiate the steps to my seat, all the while expressing concern and urging me to take care of my health. At this point, I couldn't help but think that all those hundreds of people we spoke to are responsible for our country's safety, yet they opened their hearts to make us comfortable and gave us more than ample good food. They helped our mission, to encourage young students to foster and continue their career opportunities, by opening their wallets with more than generous contributions to the Tuskegee Airmen's Youth Educational Assistance Fund.

Listed below are just a few of the wonderful F.B.I. Employees I had the pleasure of personally meeting:

Dennis R. Weaver – He now resides in Arkansas; we keep in touch with each other

Richard A. Singleton

Marty Goins

Falamie Jackson

Kathleen Walker

Darlene Butler

Madonna McGovern

Elton W. Thomas

Mark Allen – We contact each other at Christmas

Speech at the Department of Defense

United States Southern Command, Miami, Florida February 14, 2002

On February 14, 2002, it was my great pleasure to be the guest speaker at the United States Southern Command's African American History Month Celebration. I was invited by Brigadier General R. A. Huck, United States Marine Corps, Chief of Staff.

I have to say that were it not for the help of Mr. Robert "Doodie" Matthews, who was my able facilitator, I may not have been able to fulfill this engagement. It was Doodie, as we affectionately call him, who carried my luggage and saw to it that our travel was smooth, both going and returning. We were their guests for three days.

I can heartily attest to the fact that the military role as host is non-paralleled. We were met at our destination by our very gracious welcoming committee, who literally rolled out the "red carpet." The committee was comprised of the following: Lieutenant Colonel Stanley Brown, who was Deputy Director of the Southern Command; Ms. Theresa Fitzpatrick, Civilian Personnel/Equal Opportunity Officer; Ms. Nivia Butler, Deputy Chief of Protocol; and Sergeant Ryad Naseer, who arranged for all travel once we arrived at our very plush lodgings, which were located on the airport grounds. I was very impressed by the action of Ms. Butler, who spoke in Spanish to the bellhops and maids. I did not understand the exchange; however the result was that I was moved from a regular room to a suite.

The activity was held in the Headquarters main conference room. I have never seen such a grandiose auditorium. It seemed like there were over 500 service personnel in attendance. There were about 15 tables arranged directly in front of the platform where I made my presentation. Seated at these tables were the senior officers. I'm proud to report that Doodie was seated among the officers with his nameplate in front of him.

I was introduced by Master Sergeant Garrett Edmonds, who is the Assistant Executive Officer for the Chief of Staff. Sergeant Naseer cautioned me before I entered the room: "General Huck is a 'spit and polish' Marine. He has allotted you 25 minutes for your presentation."

I understood the look in the Sergeant's eyes as he turned away (Mrs. Margie Battle didn't raise no fool!). I spoke very distinctly, but with expression. I concluded at 23 minutes. Once I finished with the

Tuskegee Fight Song on my lips, the entire audience rose at once and gave me a full five-minute ovation.

General Huck made the closing remarks and presented me with a large bronze plaque, expressing the appreciation of the Southern Command for my appearance.

Galesville Gala

On Sunday, July 25, 2004, the Galesville Heritage Museum hosted an Authentic Crafts Demonstration that ran from one PM until four PM. This was a part of the South County Sundays Program, and included such traditional skills as quilting, woodworking, and spinning.

For this event, I was asked to sponsor a book signing for my autobiography, *Easier Said*. I cannot say enough about the "red carpet treatment" given to me by the following members of the Galesville Heritage Museum: Captain Jack Smith, Rever Sellman, Debra Dixon, Lois and Bill Bird, Chris Tucker, Lois Sheckells, Roberta and Dick Cossard, Gertrude Makell, and Thomas and Mrs. Tereshinski. Also, I would like to express my thanks to the owner, Jennifer Funn, and manager, Douglass David, of the Topside Inn who both graciously stopped by to meet me and purchase my book.

The mere fact that as small a community as Galesville is reaching out to former teachers, service men and women, educators, etc., is very uplifting and fruitful to those young people in their quest to carry on the rich Galesville history.

LeRoy Battle Day

Prince George's Community College, April 21, 2005

Without a doubt, one of the most meaningful, dynamic, uplifting days in my entire life occurred on Thursday, April 21, 2005.

Dr. Mary L. Brown of the Humanities and English Department at Prince George's Community College, located in Upper Marlboro,

Maryland, founded the Book Bridge Project there in 1996, and is the director. This is a campus- and community-wide reading program that brings both groups together in shared learning experiences through public forums and other activities. It uses literature as the basis for building a unique bridge between the college and the surrounding community to further multicultural understanding and improve relations with the public.

Sometime in spring 2004, Dr. Brown called and notified me that my autobiography, *Easier Said*, had been selected for the Book Bridge Project for 2004-2005.

Dr. Brown further informed me that there would be a total of six public forums and activities covering me and my book, ending on Thursday, April 21, 2005, with an "Authors' Day." Authors' Day started at 9:15 AM in front of the college gymnasium. We were treated to a performance and parade by the Frederick Douglass High School's drumline, majorettes, and flag corps (they looked splendid in their uniforms trimmed in white, maroon, and gold). Mr. Alphonso Jiles, band director, could not attend; unfortunately, there was death in his family.

In addition to their sizzling performance, it was very gratifying to observe the perfect deportment of all—definitely reflecting the brilliant leadership of Mr. Jiles.

At 10:50 AM, all gathered in the community rooms where accolades and gifts were showered on me. In addition, a young alto saxophonist named Steven Garrison regaled the audience with two difficult, yet catchy, tunes (he was the embodiment of self-esteem). Also, at this session, citations from the state and county governments, including one from the Honorable Jack B. Johnson, County Executive, Prince George's County, were read.

Also in attendance were Officials Delegate James Proctor, Prince George's County; Congressman C. A. "Dutch" Ruppersberger, Second District, Maryland; Dr. Beatrice P. Tignor,* Board Chair, Prince

George's County Public Schools; Ms. Alonia C. Sharps, Executive Assistant to the President of Prince George's Community College; and Dr. Ronald A. Williams, President of Prince George's Community College. Alumnae and alumni of Frederick Douglass High School were Mrs. Doloris Addison; Mrs. Gwendolyn "Susie" Proctor,* who also was a high-stepping drum majorette at Frederick Douglass High School; Mr. Donald G. Tolson*; Mr. Earl Tolson*; Mrs. Alice Hamilton Addison*; Mrs. Hermoine Duckett Reynolds; and Mr. Charles Dent*.

Presenting gifts were Mr. and Mrs. Elijah Thorne, Mr. and Mrs. Doloris Addison, and Mr. and Mrs. Lawrence* and Linda Newman*. Representing the Tuskegee Airmen (and looking splendid in their bright red jackets) were Mr. and Mrs. Jim and Joy Branham Pryde; Colonel Leo Gray; Colonel George "Hank" Henry; Colonel Elmer Jones, Senior Master Sergeant; Thomas "Sam" Bass; Lieutenant Bill Broadwater; and Chief Master Sergeant Clarence Turner.

Kudos to the following musicians for providing music for the awards luncheon: Professor Ned Judy, keyboard; Lawrence Melton, bassist; Greg Phillips, drums; Blake Cramer, keyboards (United States Naval Academy); Dick Glass, trumpet (United States Navy Band, Retired); Gary Kinkeby, vocalist (chair of Prince George's Community College Arts and Music); and Whit Williams, tenor sax.

Once again, my heartfelt thanks extend to Dr. Mary L. Brown, director, the Book Bridge Project, and to Mr. Leo P. Heppner, photographer.

* *The starred names are former members of the Douglass Band.*

Closing Notes

I would like to end this treatise on a resounding upbeat note. On Saturday, August 27, 2005, it was my extreme pleasure to be honored for the service and dedication I gave to my country as a Tuskegee Airman and as a teacher. I have taught in the high schools for 28 years, serving as band director, guidance counselor, and vice principal.

Throughout the bittersweet experiences, of my life, it was my time to morph gradually from early adulthood into manhood. As a young man, I was very flip at times; I railed against any act or system that I perceived to be wrong, not troubling myself to question my actions (I did what was called "shooting from the hip"). It was my experiences as a Tuskegee Airman that lifted the veil that clouded my vision and thinking.

As a Tuskegee Airman, I learned to take a stand against blatant racism. In our service, I was threatened with being shot by a white corporal armed with a 45-caliber submachine gun for just asking the guard to let our bus (which was crowded with 50 cadets—off duty, looking forward to going to town—who were roasting under the hot Texas sun) to proceed.

Not even while faced with horrible consequences, such as the threat of being sent to the stockade (military prison) or facing hanging (for being part of the "Mutiny at Freeman Field") for having the audacity to enter the White officers' club against direct orders, did my conviction waiver.

Later, as a high school teacher (band director), I pulled my band from a parade because several White marchers—dressed in ragged clown suits, made up in black-face, and carrying large bottles with "XXX" for whiskey printed in white on them—were directly in front of our band formation.

"Get that band going," the White parade marshall screamed. I shouted back, "Not until you get that garbage out of the parade ranks."

The marshall looked at me and I stared him down. He hastily called a meeting with some other White leaders. A few minutes later, I saw those individuals I had protested against leave, and thus be swallowed up in the crowd. I then turned to my lead majorette, Barbara Parker, to tell her to form the band; this was needless, however, because Barbara (always on top of her job) had already signaled the band to attention.

I spent my first 18 years of teaching at Frederick Douglass Elementary Junior Senior High School, located in Upper Marlboro, Maryland. During this tenure, Douglass bands achieved local, state, and national acclaim by outperforming other larger groups to win first place awards for Prince George's County Fire Convention Parades, state-wide Inaugural Parades, and the nationwide Cherry Blossom Parade.

After 1968, I earned my Master's Degree in education from the University of Maryland, and furthered my advanced studies by taking graduate courses in administration at Bowie State College (now a university). These studies led to my appointments as guidance counselor and, later, vice principal, until my retirement in 1978.

During my retirement, I have attended many, many affairs that recognized the retirement of teachers who unselfishly gave of themselves to their students. It was very satisfying to see and hear the wonderful accolades given to these persons. Never in my life did I expect such recognition honoring me.

However, to my utter amazement and delight, such an affair was given on August 27, 2005. The main person heading up this activity was a former member of my first band formed in 1950, Donald Gilford Tolson, Senior. Donald, along with his professional-grade committee, produced a very classy affair, which was held at the Waldorf Jaycees Center located in Waldorf, Maryland.

The committee consisted of Donald G. Tolson, Sr., Dorothea H. Smith, Cheryl Ambrose, Michele Reynolds, Tawana Hinton, Arlean Winifield, and M. Bernadette Tolson. It was extremely exhilarating to see over 400 people in attendance, consisting of former bandsmen, former coworkers, band boosters, parents, and friends.

It is said, "A teacher will never get rich teaching." I'll add that the richest feeling a teacher can have is hearing, "Hello, Mr. or Mrs. _____. Thank you for recognizing the hidden skills I had and nurturing my potential. Meet my children and spouse; we owe a lot to you."

I repeat, I'm deeply indebted to Gilford Tolson for making my dream a reality. Gilford was in a class by himself, serving as Master of Ceremonies. Everyone felt that he had missed his calling, that he should have been a standup comedian. Gilford had the audience in the palm of his hand, and they responded to each situation with laughter or quiet respect. Also, kudos to Mrs. Delores Addison for the very unique bookmarks. Delores is the wife of Thomas Addison, the talented trombone player for my early first band at Frederick Douglass Elementary Junior Senior High School.

Congressional Gold (A Few Thoughts)

On Thursday, March 29, 2007, Congress saw fit and proper to award me the Congressional Gold Medal for the heroic service (of my unit in the Tuskegee Airmen) rendered for our country during World War II. At the time, I was a young "shavetail" (Second Lieutenant), serving as a bombardier and navigator.

As I look back on this situation, I cannot but help recall that it was in the service that I became a man. When I say that, I'm talking about squaring one's shoulders and taking responsibility for one's actions, regardless of the consequences.

It was on this fateful, hot, dusty day in Texas, at the Midland Army Airfield, where as a cadet, I was headed for the airfield's entrance gate to board a bus to town and enjoy an evening of fun. A tan sports car driven by First Lieutenant Coleman Young drove up beside me, and he asked if I was headed for town. I saluted and hopped in.

When we arrived at the gate, the guard waved us on. First Lieutenant Coleman Young turned off his ignition; meanwhile, the traffic behind us got really long. The guard came over to Lieutenant Young and said, "I waved you on through."

Lieutenant Young looked at him with cold eyes and said, "You don't salute officers?"

The guard said lamely, "I thought you were a cadet."

Lieutenant Young shouted, "Well, you can see I'm an officer now!" With that, he took hold of the guard's collar and said, "If you don't have enough respect to salute the man, then salute this silver bar." And the guard popped to attention, saluted and passed us on.

That scene burned in my mind like a hot iron. I vowed then and there that if I truly believed in something that I would "got to the wall" taking a stand. This belief served me well during the "Freeman Field Mutiny." I knew I was right and was willing to die for my cause. My credo is "right is right if nobody's right, and wrong is wrong if everybody's wrong."

I think it's a pity that so many men and women go through life never really having to put their beliefs to the ultimate test.

Speech by Original Tuskegee Airman
LeRoy A. Battle

Saint Michaels Lutheran Church
Mitchellville, Maryland, Saturday, June 16, 2007

I'm very honored and, if the truth be known, very flattered to be in this role as an active participant for this august occasion. I will attempt to briefly encapsulate the project known as the Tuskegee experience into three parts.

1941: The First Wave

It was the best of times when all agreed, World War II was a war worth fighting. All of the talented, brightest young White men enlisted or were drafted into the United States Army Air Corps and were given an equal opportunity to succeed or fail in their quest of earning gold bars and silver wings.

It was the worst of times because the most gifted and brightest Black youth were denied access into the military aviation program. However, the Black community—along with powerful, sympathetic Whites and the Black press, including *The Pittsburgh Courier*, *The Chicago Defender*, *The New York Amsterdam News*, and *The Afro-American*, to name a few— waged a valiant, persistent, and effective struggle against the government. These groups urged the removal of all obstacles that prohibited Blacks from entering the military flying program.

At that time, there were only five Black officers in all of the military branches. They were Benjamin O. Davis, Sr., Benjamin O. Davis, Jr., and three army chaplains.

The Tuskegee experience was started in 1941 by the government, despite strong resistance from key political policy makers and most officials in the war department. The government agreed to start a test program destined to train Blacks in all aspects of military aviation with the stimulation that should said program prove successful, the unit would only be deployed on a segregated basis. There was no doubt in their collective minds that this experiment would fail, but they kept their hidden agenda under wraps. After all, everybody knew that "Colored folk" were inferior to Whites, and in no shape, form, or manner could they master the skills needed to fly airplanes.

The Tuskegee Airmen owe a huge debt of gratitude to Mrs. Eleanor Roosevelt, who visited the Tuskegee Institute in March 1940 to check out the civilian pilot training program directed by the founder, Chief Alfred Anderson, a Black pilot.

The secret service detail guarding Mrs. Roosevelt almost had a collective baby when she requested that Chief Anderson take her up for a spin. As a direct result of her experiences at the Tuskegee Institute, Mrs. Roosevelt became a very vocal advocate of Blacks participating in the aviation program. She made it her personal mission to state the case for Blacks in aviation to her husband, Franklin Delano Roosevelt, then President of the United States. And, in particular, she urged the establishment of a complete flying school at Tuskegee Institute, one that would take the cadets from primary through advanced training.

The President agreed and immediately used his good office to see that $75,000 be given as seed money to clear the densely wooded area to construct what we know now as Moton Field. The contract was awarded to Black architect and contractor McKissack and McKissack (father and daughter). The work of constructing the airfield began on July 23, 1941.

The first class of Negro flying cadets was started in July 1941. This class was composed of 12 trainees and one student officer, Captain Benjamin O. Davis, Jr. Captain Davis had graduated from West Point in 1936. He was a very, very special man who endured, yet prevailed, under the most despicable, horrible conditions in order to gain his commission.

Only five of the 13 completed the course and received their wings and commissions on March 7, 1942. It wasn't until April 1943 that the

99th Pursuit Squadron—consisting of 26 pilots and commanded by then Lieutenant Colonel Benjamin O. Davis, Jr.—were deployed to North Africa for combat duty with the 33rd fighter group.

There they met with hostility from their group commander and, on their first mission, were not coupled with experienced pilots nor in any way briefed on the "Rules of Engagement," as was the procedure practiced with new White pilots on their first mission. In short, the commander wrote the Tuskegee Airmen up as not fit to be in combat due to lack of skills.

There was a hue and cry to disband the 99th and send them home. However, a passionate plea by Benjamin O. Davis, Jr., persuaded the naysayers to give the Tuskegee Airmen another chance. The 99th was transferred to the 79th group, led by a non-bigoted commander.

While Lieutenant Colonel Davis was still stateside, the 99th fell under the command of Captain George "Spanky" Roberts. On the morning of January 27, 1944, with 15 pilots flying the obsolescent P-40s, the Tuskegee Airmen met a large number of Germans flying the much superior Focke-Wulf 190s, and yet the 99th shot down six Focke-Wulfs and damaged another four.

That same afternoon, three more Focke-Wulfs were shot down. The next day, January 28th, the Tuskegee Airmen shot down four more German fighters. Yes, in 1941, the United States' government did not want Blacks to fly, but in 1944, the Nazis did not want Blacks to fly!!!

1944: The Second Wave

On July 3rd, 1944, the 332nd fighter group was formed. This consisted of four fighter squadrons: the 99th, 100th, 301st, and 302nd. The 332nd fighter pilots knew that the future of Negroes in military aviation depended upon their performance. To its credit, the government at last conceded and admitted that Negro fighter pilots had proven to be worthy of the name—they gave the 332nd the high performance P-47

Thunderbolt. It did not matter what plane the Tuskegee Airmen flew, they always outscored the Luftwaffe. Finally, they were assigned the P-51 Mustang, the best fighter developed by the United States during World War II.

On June 25th, the Tuskegee Airmen again showed their mettle when Captain Wendell O. Pruitt and Lieutenant Gwynne Pierson teamed up to sink a German destroyer, using only their .50 caliber machine guns — they were returning to base from a bombing raid and had no bombs left.

It was the 332nd group that decided to paint their spinners and tails red, thus starting the name and tradition of "Red Tails." The Germans called them "The Red-Tailed Devils." It wasn't long before they were assigned to bomber escort duty.

At first the bomb groups were reluctant to use them, believing the "old wives tale" that Blacks could not fly or "cut it." However, it did not take long for the records to show that all bombers escorted to and from the targets by the Red Tails returned to base with no losses due to enemy fighter action! Altogether, the 332nd fighter group escorted our bombers for over 200 missions and never lost one due to enemy fighters! This was no accident, as Colonel Davis insisted that fighters stay with the bombers and not go chasing off for individual kills; they formed an umbrella over the bombers.

This news spread quickly. Soon, most of the bomber groups were requesting the Red Tails to escort them. Through hundreds of attacks and amidst the heaviest defenses, the Tuskegee Airmen challenged and bested the elite of the German Luftwaffe.

To give you a better idea of the fortitude, tenacity, and downright determination of the Red Tails, I'll describe the joint mission of March 24, 1945. The 332nd was called upon to take part in a cooperative mission with five other fighter groups to escort bombers over Berlin. This was a maximum effort mission. The 332nd assignment was to rendezvous with the bombers at Brux, about 150 miles south of Berlin.

On the way, they were met by a gaggle of ME 109s. The 332nd quickly dispatched them and continued on to Brux, having used up precious fuel and ammunition.

The main mission of the 332nd was to escort bombers to the Initial Point (I.P.) at the edge of the city. The target for the bombers was the Daimler-Benz tank assembly plant, the most heavily protected target in the Third Reich. This assignment was a very high honor for the 332nd as well as an indication of the respect and confidence that the high command had finally developed for the Tuskegee Airmen.

The I.P. is the most dangerous part of a bombing mission. The plane must fly a straight course, maintaining the same airspeed and altitude in order for the bombardier to enter the correct stats into the Norden Bombsight. The 332nd fighter group was supposed to have been relieved at the I.P. by another fighter group; the relieving unit failed to make the rendezvous.

Despite low fuel and ammunition, the 332nd elected to stay with the bombers. As the bombers started their bomb run, they were attacked by another formation of Germany's newest jet fighters, the ME 262 jets. By mission's end, the Red Tails shot down three German jets and damaged another six, while losing only one P-51. Captain Roscoe Brown shot down the first jet.

1945: The Third Wave

The Third Wave deals with the 477th Medium Bombardment Group, of which I was a bombardier/navigator in the 616th squadron. Our mantra was: "Stay focused, stick-to-it, get it done." The B-25 Billy Mitchell Medium Bomber was our assigned weapon.

In the European theatre of war, the 332nd fighter group was proving for all to see that the Black man was very capable of navigating and precisely handling his fast plane, maneuvering it at terrific speeds in actual combat, mastering the technique of accurately directing fire in aerial dogfights, and exercising split-second judgment in unexpected situations and emergencies.

Back home, there was another fight against blatant and abject racism in the armed forces being actively fought against by the men who comprised the 477th Medium Bombardment Group.

On April 5th, 1945, these bombardiers, pilots, and navigators— officers all—took part in what is known as the "Freeman Field Mutiny," located in Seymour, Indiana (Selfridge Field).

It began April 1, 1945, when the base commander, upon learning that a large contingent of Negro pilots, navigators, and bombardiers would immediately be assigned to his largely White command for intense combat training, issued a letter segregating trainees from base and supervisory officers. (At the time, all the designated trainees were Black, and all base and supervisory personnel were White.)

Four days after posting the letter, the commander heard that some newly arrived Negro officers would try to enter the officer's club, so he ordered all doors locked except the main entrance. He then posted armed military police at the entrance, with orders to keep out "non-members."

That night, 18 other Black officers and I tried to enter the club. We were immediately placed under arrest and under armed guards, some with Thompson .45 caliber machine guns. We were led back to our quarters. Prior to this, Bill Terry, a tall strapping twin-engine pilot, brushed against a superior officer to gain entrance and was subsequently charged and court-martialed for assault.

During this period of arrest and interrogation, the base commander issued a letter stating that all charges would be dropped against any officer who would sign a letter that stated that the signee agreed not to enter the officers' club again. All 101 of us really bonded together and refused to sign. I made up my mind—I had a very serious talk with my heavenly father and committed myself to fight against the injustice or die!

During my arrest, I was visited by two full colonels from the Inspector General's office as requested by the Secretary of War Stimson. I was called out around two AM and directed to a small room with just one bright light bulb, a desk, and three folding chairs.

The interrogation lasted for about one hour; two points stuck in my mind:

1. *They wanted to know who our leaders were.*

2. *One officer bellowed at me, "Lieutenant, are you aware that, by refusing to obey a direct order from a senior officer in the time of war, you could be sentenced to the stockade or, worse, that you could be hung?"*

This was pretty heady stuff for a young shave-tail. At that time, another officer said, "We're ready to swear you in as a hostile witness under oath." And with that, he read the pertinent articles of war to me, as outlined in army regulations, and intense interrogation followed.

The downside of this situation was that the efficiency of the 477th Medium Bombardment Group was temporarily destroyed. Meanwhile, there was a hue and cry of Black newspapers and parents (my mother wrote to President Truman).

Colonel Selway was removed as base commander, and Colonel Benjamin O. Davis, Jr., was recalled from the European theatre of war to take charge. This was the first time the 477th was commanded by a Black senior officer.

General George C. Marshall ordered our release from arrest. We were then again sent to Walterboro Air Force Base in South Carolina for further over-water training in preparation to being sent to the Pacific theatre of war. Colonel Davis reorganized the 477th into a composite group by eliminating squadrons 616 and 619, and adding the 99th fighter squadron.

Since my squadron, the 616th, was eliminated, I was permitted to return to Tuskegee and enroll in the pilot training program. At this venture, things were moving at quite a rapid pace. I had passed the pre-flight stage and was entering the primary phase.

On August 6th, the atom bomb was dropped on Hiroshima, Japan. On August 9th, another nuclear device was dropped on Nagasaki, Japan.

I was the lead plane on a cross-country flight when I heard that the war department had released a directive, stating that all officers who had accrued enough points and had a certain M.O.S. (Military Occupational Specialty) number could opt for "early out." I immediately returned to base, hurried to the administration building, and filed my papers for release.

On November 7th, 1945, I was honorably discharged from the United States Army Air Corps. On August 12, 1995 (50 years later), thanks to the persistent, untiring efforts on the part of Lieutenant Colonel James C. Warren—to eradicate the United States government's terrible wrong in the "Freeman Field Mutiny"—and to the most positive response and cooperation on the part of the Honorable Rodney A. Coleman, the then assistant secretary of the Air Force, in Atlanta, Georgia, Mr. Coleman announced that the letters of reprimand would be expunged from the records of those who would request same in writing.

Air Force Chief of Staff General Ronald R. Fogleman presented Warren and Terry with official documents expunging their records, and overturning the court martial verdict that had convicted Roger Terry.

Lastly, I'll sing with pride the 99th fight song:

Contact contact
Joy stick back
Sailing through the blue
Loyal sons of the 99th. Brave and tried and true
For we are heroes—day or night
To hell with the axis might
Fight fight fight fight
Fighting 99th

God Bless!!!

PART V

CONCLUSION

Thoughts and Thanks

In retrospect, it would be wonderful if I could relive and redo those experiences that would reflect me in a more favorable light. However, the reality of the situation says in very clear tones that, "It is very, very difficult to unring a bell."

So I, unashamedly, face the world with a steady eye and firm step always towards a promising future. As I regretfully finish *And the Beat Goes On*, I should like to pay thanks and tribute to the following members of my immediate family.

My Family

My very dear mother, Margie Battle-Smith, who passed away November 11, 2006, after living 103 years young. It is a wonderful blessing from our good Lord that Mother had all of her God-given faculties until she was gone; she could hold her own in conversation, thinking, and problem solving with anyone on most topics. I will always thank her for my genes.

My wife Alice, or Princess, as we lovingly call her, is the inspiration and source of my hopes, dreams, and spirit to press on, regardless of formidable obstacles that constantly confront me. Alice also serves as in-house editor of *And the Beat Goes On* and my other writing.

My son, Terry Battle, from my first marriage, who is an outstanding professional musician who performs with numerous jazz greats both in America and abroad.

My daughter, Lisa P. Battle-Singletary, M.D., who in addition to plying her trade at Johns Hopkins hospital, is also an accomplished musician in her own right. She also gave me the priceless gift of proofreading this book for me.

My son, LeRoy A. Battle, Jr., who also thrives as a performing instrumentalist and music teacher. He has led bands on the Jay Leno and P. Diddy shows. LeRoy is also the director of three church choirs.

The most precious jewels, however, are my three grandchildren who never fail to bring me joy: LeRoy III, eight years; Sydney, seven years; and Justice, three years.

Kimberly Battle, wife of LeRoy, Jr., is the wonderful mother of the precious jewels in the crown. Kim is very wise beyond her young years. Nephew Forrest

I'd like to say a word or two about my wife's nephew, Forrest Holt. The following situation occurred about the mid-1960s. I was vice principal at the Frederick Douglass Elementary Junior Senior High School in Upper Marlboro, Maryland. It was springtime and love was in the air. Well, it so happened that during a particular week in April, the buses were involved in significant traffic slow downs, which affected parents coming and going to drop off their children for morning classes at the school.

Our principal, Mr. Robert F. Frisby, called me to his office one Tuesday morning and said, "Mr. Battle, there is a serious problem involving the timely flow of the school buses. I want the problem to go away."

"Yes sir," I replied, and walked to the front of the white line where the buses usually lined up. I thought there was something peculiar because the bus was double-parked in the driveway. Then I spotted it: a dark-colored car to the right of the bus. I quickly ran up to the driver's side of the car and was about to shout. However, all I could see was the side of a male student and his arm was embracing a female student. It was clear to see, as Clint Eastwood put it, that they were exchanging "spit." I banged on the window and shouted, "Roll this damn window down, now." Lo and behold, it was my wife's nephew Forrest, who faced me with a very sheepish grin. Well, needless to say, I sent the young lady scurrying to class and I reamed out Forrest, ending with "and I never want to see you around here anymore; you don't even go to this school!"

I'm happy to report that the traffic flowed smoothly from that day on. The problem occurred because the young bus driver was an acquaintance of Forrest. I got a promise from him that he would never let this situation happen again.

A few years later, the genius side of Forrest came out. Forrest's father, Jimmy Holt, was far and wide considered to be the finest welder in Maryland. Jimmy always was involved with very heavy equipment. Well, one morning, he permitted a friend of his to operate this monstrous machine known as a trash compactor. This compactor was easily twice as large as a front-end loader and much more complicated to operate. As it happened, this fellow somehow got his wires crossed, the machine caught fire, and all the electrical wires and connections were destroyed. For two months the machine just sat there at the mercy of the weather. Jimmy was getting to the point of being willing to sell the remains for junk.

One morning, I looked out my door and saw Forrest climbing over the machine and making notes. "What can he do?" I asked myself.

Several days later, after observing Forrest, I saw him take out a notebook, tape measure, and he didn't not stop until the complete machine was measured, inside and out. Then, later that day, I saw Forrest with electrical coils of various colors. And so the scenario continued for approximately six weeks and then, lo and behold, one morning I awakened to the eardrum shattering sound of a powerful motor accompanying a crashing sound. I rushed to the door to see what was happening. There was Forrest, operating the compactor and driving towards me. Without plans or schematics, Forrest had rewired the compactor's electrical system, and he did it all by himself.

To this day, Forrest has been performing miracles with his hands for others. There isn't any problem electrical or mechanical that I've seen that he couldn't solve. He is my right-hand man who makes sure everything is taken care of; he gets me where I need to go. Alice and I both owe quite a bit to Forrest and his lovely wife, Shirley, who can best be described as an "Earth Angel," for all the good that she does.

Alice's Friends

I would like to take this opportunity to thank the following beautiful ladies for their special friendship to my wife, Alice.

Alice chairs the United Methodist Church's volunteer office for the Southern Region of Maryland. Once a month, Alice and her loyal committee, consisting of Mrs. Thelma Howard, Mrs. Isabelle Estep, Mrs. Credella Matthews, Mrs. Matilda Fletcher, and Mrs. Patricia Gross, all travel to Columbia, Maryland, where the headquarters of the United Methodist Church is located.

The committee begins work around 8:30 AM and, by five PM, they will have stuffed and mailed several thousand fliers, which contain very important information from the Bishop to the members of the Church.

Other Significant People in My Life

Mrs. Bernadette Tolson—A very caring person. Bernadette's role in making my Tribute on August 27, 2005, was one that held the various activities together. Bernadette works out of Mayor Anthony Williams' office in Washington. It is with acute knowledge and contacts that she is able to move things along effectively.

The Woods, Madeline and Phillip, are very loyal and helpful friends who always made it their business to see to the comfort of my family by shopping and cleaning for my mother while she was alive.

Delydia and Calvin Jones, who I call "Earth Angels," because both my wife and I are wheelchair-bound. Delydia has taken it upon herself to do the much needed "grocerin'" for us each and every week.

You know one hardly ever thinks about the ordinary, mundane, yet most important things that make for a smooth transition of life due to handicaps. With this in mind, I'd like to make a loud shout out to my brother-in-law, Thomas Claude Holt and his lovely wife, Dorothy. Rain or shine, Claude is punctual with our mail. Also, he picks up our prescriptions, all with a big, warm smile. Then there is Ms. Cheryl Luttrell, a retired Capitol Hill police officer who has been welcomed into our family. When asked, Cheryl never fails to answer our call to take or pickup articles from the cleaners, deliver messages, or the like.

Alice and I are extremely grateful to the wonderful owner and employees of Rennos' Market in Shady Side, Maryland: Mr. Mohan Grover, who is the "Mayor" of Shady Side, his lovely wife Ish, and Cordell Salisbury, the greatest butcher anywhere. Time and time again, Mr. Grover invites me to speak at public celebrations held in Shady Side. Mr. Grover sponsors activities free of charge to the people of Shady Side. He provides the food, drink (sodas), and entertainment while teaching public safety habits that promote life-saving techniques regarding fires and fire hazards.

Dennis "Tank" Davis—Kept the light of survival bright.

Martin Carroll—A friend indeed.

Dr. Mary Brown—A person with a true vision of hope.

Katherine Burke—No problem is too small or too large for her to handle.

Tony Kornheiser—A loyal friend to the end.

Michael Wilbon—Staff writer for *The Washington Post*; he is the truth!!!

Then there is Joy Branham-Pryde, along with her Tuskegee Airman husband Jim. They spend their time in the field with sleeves rolled up, perspiration dripping from their chins, toiling to see that the Gala Luncheon (for example) is a rousing fund-raising success—all for the benefit of the Youth Educational Assistance Fund of the East Coast Chapter Tuskegee Airmen, Inc. They are always there to answer my queries as I write.

Along with the above kudos, I'm compelled, yet happy to mention Sam Bass, a totally unselfish Tuskegee Airman whose personal mission is to help others.

Tess Spooner (gorgeous) wife of Major General Richard Spooner— Tess was National President of the Tuskegee Airmen and has the heart to match the office. She is my mentor.

Major (Retired) William "Bill" Peterson—A trusted friend who "tells-it-like-it is" and expects the same from you.

Robert and Elaine Matthews—Both "Doodie" Robert and Elaine have been trusted and dependable friends to Alice and me. Elaine served as secretary for Alice at Shady Side Elementary School, along with Peggy Tucker and Naomi Holland-Dennis. A hearty shout out goes to Elaine, who, in addition to typing and making sense of my garbled notes, serves as an in-house editor. I am extremely grateful to her for her untiring efforts and appropriate contributions towards a successful fruition of *And the Beat Goes On*. Doodie has been (and still is) responsible for extending my professional playing life by driving me to my gigs and loading my drums.

Henry Cooley—A former Airman who always calls to check on my well being.

Dorothea Smith—A former teacher who is a real "self-starter." Dorothea is very instrumental in lining up speaking engagements for me; I thank her for her constant support.

Jean Queen Haughton—I am always thankful for your friendship and tenacity.

Vivian Truxon—Was one of my first majorettes (1950). Vivian was very effect in promoting my first book throughout Charles County.

The following former bandsmen and their wives/husbands honored me by traveling over 75 miles to hear my band, The Altones, perform at Harford Community College: Lawrence Newman (baritone horn) and wife, Linda; Tom Addison (trombone) and wife, Delores;

Jim Harley (trumpet) and wife, Viola; Alice Hamilton Addison (baritone horn) and husband, Joseph.

Warrick Hill—My classmate at Morgan State College, a very renowned author in his own right. He wrote *Before Us Lies the Timber.*

Gilford Tolson, or "Groucho" as we lovingly call him, has been one of the stabilizing influences in my teaching career. He is a true self-starter. He has also demonstrated to me that people can disagree without being disagreeable.

Mozella Harris thinks of ways to cheer you up. It is wonderful when she will "pop up" without announcement with a delicious Subway sandwich.

Irma Howard has been a lifelong acquaintance who has proven to be a loving, dependable friend to our family.

Dr. Ida Clark always answers the call when my wife or I have need. It is the many things she does that means so much to us.

Mable Thompson—Words cannot describe the love and attention she brings to any meeting (chance or planned). Mable is willing to help with her larger-than-life smile.

Alice Garrett and her family are like "one" with us. If my wife, Alice, has a bad time (because of her illness, multiple sclerosis), Alice Garrett is there with complete meals and love.

Colonel George Henry—We call him "Mr. Stagecoach" because he picks up members who do not have transportation to attend meetings and functions.

Romcesa Estep—A kind, caring lady who visibly demonstrates her concern and love for my family by sharing treats from the oven.

Reverend Darnell Easton and his lovely wife Margo were always on hand to show their love for my mother before and after she passed away.

Marie and Henry Jones—Always helped my wife Alice with transportation to church, sharing God's bounty from their garden.

Tina Brown, Violet Owens and her husband Hilliary always come to the aid of my family.

Elsie and Harry Brown could always be counted upon to assist Alice whenever needed.

Orma and Bill Caves—Among the finest people I ever met.

Peter and Peggy Alex—Both wonderful friends who never fail to show their love and kindness to my family.

Ray and Marva Rogers were my "old" bowling partners. In addition, Ray is a genius with electrical problems. He has been an invaluable help to us.

Marguerite Simpson—This lovely lady and I taught together at the Frederick Douglass Elementary Junior Senior High School. In addition, Marguerite loaned me several early additions of Douglass yearbooks, which enabled me to place accurate facts in my autobiographies.

Mozella Lawing—A truly unselfish pretty lady with a technical mind. She always did her best to help the Douglass "Eagle" Band.

Nancy Quander—A hard-working core teacher who spoke at the new Douglass dedication. Mrs. Quander also was quite active in raising funds for the Douglass band.

Preston Davis, Sr.—A fellow Tuskegee Airman who always calls me to keep me in "the loop."

Barbara Tongue and Ruth Ann Williams—I shall always be grateful to them for their loving care of my mother and Alice.

Moses Randall and his lovely wife Marvel—Since my disability, Moses has taken it upon himself to mow and manicure our house shrubbery.

General Robert C. Gaskill, Sr.—I'm deeply grateful to General Gaskill for permitting g me to use his good name when I contacted service agencies about broadening my book's availability.

LeRoy Beeler—Kudos to Mr. Beeler for his untiring efforts, which contributed to the success of the Tuskegee Airmen, Inc.

Thomas and Deloris Addison—A "class act," if there ever was one.

Edna F. Downey—We grew up together in Brooklyn, New York, from the late 1930s to 1940s. Out of the blue, Edna called me, after 50 years, to say she read about me being a Tuskegee Airman. She said she couldn't believe it because, on numerous trips to Coney Island, I refused to go on the roller coaster, saying it was too high for me.

Lawrence Thomas—A long-haul interstate driver who went to the Tuskegee Institute in Alabama and took photos of all old and new buildings there. The wonderful thing was, he showed me several pictures of the famed Emories where other Tuskegee Air Cadets and I were assigned sleeping quarters. He said he went there out of respect for me.

Colonel Taro Jones—This is one very smart man; I'll never forget his kindness.

Thomas "Whit" Williams and his lovely wife, Ethel—There was a time when several members of my combo group, "The Altones," passed away. I had to fill those places with quality personnel. Whit Williams on tenor sax stepped in and the Altones soared to newer heights.

I tip my hat to Thomas and Delores Proctor—They never fail to answer my call when I need them.

The following dear people have a very special place in my heart: Janie Moore Gholston, Dora Holton, Bob Price, Ethel Griffith, Elaine Blackwell, John and Daisy Myles.

Colonel Frank Herrelko and his lovely wife Edith—I'm very grateful to Frank because he always clips articles about Negro military officers and forwards them to me. Frank's son David was a brigadier general who invited me to speak at the Air Space Museum in Ohio for Negro history week.

Colonel Oliver Carter—Past president of the East Coast Chapter. A straight shooter; he walks and talks like a man.

A very special "shout-out" to the following:

Leo P. Heppner—Who never hesitated to give his photographic skills.

Charlotte Stokes—A true educational visionary.

Phyllis Ervin Evans—A future principal; the students and teachers under her guidance will be blessed with the true way.

Eloyce Ervin—When I was a struggling band director in the 1950s, she was there for me in the Band Boosters Club.

Jane Hitchcock—A wonderful author who uses her technical prowess to seek out the criminal mind and protect the public.

Sarah Sherman McGrail—I'm eternally grateful to her giving me a helping hand in my time of need; she knows the publishing procedure.

Esme McTighe—Her Editor skills kept me focused.

Donna L. Adams—She is a true beautiful jewel in the crown; a wonderful hairstylist who picks up my wife every other week and drives her to the salon to do her hair.

Catherine Anne Dixon—She is the rural letter carrier for Harwood, Maryland. She knows how difficult it is for Alice and me to get to the mailbox. Hence, she always delivers our packages with special mail.

Dr. Stephen B. Hiltabidle—Our family surgeon, who used his professional skills to operate on me and fix it so that I am able to live life with a minimum of inconvenience.

Dr. Wayne Bierbaum—Who graciously added me to his very full docket in order to help me to travel five miles to his office rather than 40 miles to another physician.

Judy Moore—Who wrote about me and was instrumental in my being inducted into the Maryland Music Educators' Hall of Fame.

Jan Stocklinski—Definitely "had my back" when I was vice principal at Suitland junior High, which enabled me to carry out my missions of keeping the school calm and orderly.

Mr. and Mrs. Harry and Claretta Wingo—Both are dear friends; they always assist my wife Alice with transportation needs.

Mr. and Mrs. Charles and Melba McMillan—They are both "Jewels in the Crown."

Mrs. Joy Anderson—Constant friend and bowling team member.

Mr. and Mrs. Henry and Electa Holland—Friends to the end!!!

Mr. Dick Christopher—Manages the "Food-Rite" store in Deale, Maryland; he reaches out in friendship to all.

Mrs. Anne Randall and her pilot husband have proven to be great friends. Ann was one of my first majorettes in 1950 at Douglass Jr. Sr. High.

Mark and Teresa Allen—When I first spoke at the FBI headquarters, Mark and Teresa gave me their wonderful support.

Helen and Mary Butler—Two aces make them wonderful friends.

Phillip and Rachel Brown—Friends; need I say more?

Ann C. Proctor, Julia Proctor Jackson, C. Silvia Proctor, Marion Walls—Special friends who made LeRoy A. Battle Day a dream come true!

Mrs. Corrine "Dimples" Boyd—Her husband Gordon Boyd, a former Tuskegee Airman, is deceased.

Delores Smith—Former teacher with me at Douglass.

Elaine Proctor Blackwell—Former teacher at Douglass.

Barry McCullough—Professor at Prince George's County Community College.

Alex "Mojo" Garrett—Former "Little Leaguer" who now helps me with walking exercises.

Paul and Jean Haughton—Author and teacher, and family friends.

John E. Deasy, Ph.D.—Superintendent of Prince George's County Public Schools.

Gwendolyn "Susie" Proctor—Former Douglass High majorette.

Mr. Rudolph Saunders—Frederick Douglass High School Principal.

Mr. Wilbert Hawkins—Former Douglass teacher and good friend of LeRoy.

Elizabeth Campeau, Chief Master Sergeant—A true professional who guided the Tuskegee Airmen at the Air Force 60th Anniversary concert where they were guests of honor.

Robert Stubbe, cameraman—Filmed the 60th Air Force Band concert. He was gracious enough to include shots of me shedding a tear when the band played, "I Can Fly... Let Me Try."

Oliver Tucker—He comes to my house to give me haircuts. He is an old-fashioned barber who still uses a straight-edge razor.

Clifton Sharps—He brings my mail every day with the daily paper.

Errol Brown—He and his parents, Phillip and Rachel, always do their best to elevate and foster Negro pride.

Dr. Louis Kofi Essandoh—A truly great heart physician.

Ernest Nick—A world-class carpenter and long-time friend.

George Padgett—A world-class plumber and true friend.

Mrs. Gay Spicer Topper—A former Douglass Eagle Bandsmen with a loving, caring heart.

Mrs. Nancy Johnson and Mrs. Norma Jenkins—These ladies are truly "jewels in the crown." They look after Alice and me as if we were their parents.

Cynthia Carter—A long-time true and loyal friend.

Jerry Burton—Chairman of the Tuskegee Airmen Speakers' Bureau, who truly encourages the Tuskegee Airmen to actively participate in all related affairs.

Fran Blacker—A long-time family friend who is now an amazing caretaker and advocate for Alice. She is an Angel sent from above!

Demitrious Pitt—A very caring person.

Membership, East Coast Chapter of Tuskegee Airmen, Incorporated

1. Lieutenant Colonel Bruce C. Alexander
2. Captain Harvey R. Alexander
3. Captain Charles W. Anderson
4. Ernest C. Anderson
5. Mr. Leon Armour, Sr.
6. Mr. Norman Artis

7.   Dr. Henri L. Bailey III

8.   Colonel Shelby G. Ball

9.   Mr. Harold G. Banks

10.   Mr. Thomas Sam Bass, Jr.

11.   Mr. LeRoy A. Battle, Sr.

12.   Mr. Robert J. Beatson

13.   Chief Master Sergeant Ronald Beckett

14.   Mr. Samuel Becton

15.   Colonel Philip G. Benjamin II

16.   Dr. Sylvanus G. Bent

17.   Major (Retired) William H. Bethel, Jr.

18.   Ms. Roberta E. Bolen

19.   Captain (Retired) John W. Booker

20.   Captain Ronald K. Booker

21.   Mrs. Corrine S. Boyd

22.   M General John A. Bradley

23.   Major Marc C. Branche

24.   Ms. Joy L. Branham-Pryde

25.   Ms. Lorine E. Brewer

26.   Mr. Madison Broadnax

27.   Mr. William E. Broadwater

28.   Brigadier General (Retired) Elmer T. Brooks

29.   Mr. Phillip W. Broome

30.   Major Charles M. Brown

31.   Lieutenant Colonel Charles Q. Brown, Jr.

32.   Major General (Retired) John M. Brown, Sr.

33.   Mrs. La Frances Brown

34.   Sergeant Lafayette Brown, Jr.

35.   Dr. Walter H. Brown, Jr.

36.   Lieutenant Colonel Mical R. Bruce

37.   Owen D. Bruce

38.   Shirley M. Buie

39.   Sergeant Major Bryan K. Burton

40.   Dr. Cyril O. Byron, Sr.

41.   Lieutenant Colonel (Retired) Simon L. Cain

42.   Reginald Campbell, Sr.

43.   Lieutenant Colonel Oliver C. Carter

44.   Colonel (Retired) Paul A. Carter

45.   Dr. Conrad H. Cheek, Sr.

46.   Lieutenant Commander (Retired) Charles O. Chisley II

47.   Mr. Leonard E. Chivis

48.   Major General Thomas E. Clifford

49.   Mr. David H. Cole

50.   Honorable Rodney A. Coleman

51.   Lieutenant Colonel (Retired) James R. Coles, Jr.

52.   Lieutenant General (Retired) John B. Conaway

53.   Mr. James Cooper

54.   Dr. F. Jane Cotton

55.   Captain (Retired) Elias W. Covington

56.   Mrs. Rosemary F. Crockett, Ph.D.

57.   Lieutenant Colonel (Retired) Woodrow W. Crockett

58.   John C. Curry

59.   Mr. Lemuel Rodney Cutis

60.   Lieutenant Colonel Clarence W. Dart

61.   Mr. Warren L. Dart

62.   Lieutenant Colonel (Retired) Ernest H. Davenport

63.   Mrs. Frances J. Davis

64.   Mr. Preston A. Davis, Sr.

65.   Mr. Preston A Davis, Jr.

66.   Honorable Ruby B. DeMesme

67.   Colonel William A. DeShields

68.   Major (Retired) Ronald Dickens

69. Mr. Crawford B. Dowdell

70. Lieutenant Colonel (Retired) Esmer L. Durham, Jr.

71. Mr. Percival W. Dyer II

72. Colonel William H. Eaton

73. Lieutenant Colonel Chiquita Y. N. English

74. Lieutenant Colonel Nelson W. English

75. Mr. Nelson E. Evans, Jr.

76. Mr. Herven P. Exum

77. Mr. William T. Fauntroy, Jr.

78. Joseph F. Ferguson, Jr.

79. Mr. Earnest P. Fingers

80. Mr. Charles H. Flowers II

81. Colonel (Retired) Aaron B. Floyd

82. Mrs. Antoinette R. Frederick

83. Colonel (Retired) Michael E. Freeman

84. Mr. Larry A. Frelow, Sr.

85. Major Eugene W. Garges, Jr.

86. Mr. Winston S. Gaskins

87. Mr. Ramon E. Gilead

88. Lieutenant Colonel Derek P. Green

89. Mr. Willie E. Greene

90. Colonel (Retired) Frederick D. Gregory

91. Dr. Alan L. Gropman

92. Mr. Henry J. Hall

93. Mr. Leonard C. Hall, Jr.

94. Dr. Deborah Hall-Greene

95. Dr. Victor L. Hancock

96. Brigadier General John B. Handy

97. Chief Master Sergeant (Retired) Joseph L. Hardy, Sr.

98. Mr. Donald L. Harper

99. Reverend Hiram H. Haywood, Jr.

100. Mr. Stewart S. Henley

101. Colonel (Retired) George A. Henry, Jr.

102. Colonel (Retired) Burl E. Hickman

103. Major Sergeant (Retired) Robert L. Higgenbotham

104. Mr. Thurman Higginbotham

105. Major General (Retired) Johnny J. Hobbs

106. Major Sergeant (Retired) Jerome Hodge

107. Mr. Andrew B. Holloway, Sr.

108. Mr. Charles R. Holmes, Jr.

109. Mr. Clarence Holmes

110. Mrs. Judith W. Holton

111. Mr. William F. Holton

112. Colonel (Retired) Hunter S. Hopson, Jr.

113. Commander Ernest Huckaby

114. Dr. Charles H. Hunter

115. Mr. William H. Hymes, Sr.

116. Brigadier General (Retired) Reginald K. Ingram, Sr.

117. Mr. Nathaniel K. Jackson

118. Mr. Phillip R. Jackson

119. Mr. Walter Jackson III

120. Mr. Julius C. Jefferson

121. Colonel (Retired) William J. Jefferson, Jr.

122. Brigadier General (Retired) Charles B. Jiggetts

123. Mr. Hampton E. Johnson

124. Technical Sergeant Haywood L. Johnson

125. Mr. Arnette A. Jones

126. Lieutenant Colonel Conell Jones

127. Colonel (Retired) Conway B. Jones, Jr.

128. Colonel (Retired) Elmer D. Jones

129. Mr. Eric M. Jones

130. Mr. Herbert H. Jones, Jr.

131. Leroy Jones, Jr.

132. Lieutenant Colonel Prentice E. Jones

133. Colonel Taro K. Jones

134. Dr. William Kate, Jr.

135. Bruce R. Kendall

136. Mrs. Valerie L. Kendall

137. John H. Kershaw

138. Chief Master Sergeant Franklin Killebrew

139. Lieutenant Colonel Sheila M. King-Coleman

140. Ms. Mable M. Knott

141. Mr. Gilbert B. Langford

142. Mrs. E. Theophia H. Lee

143. Dr. Nancy Leftenant-Colon

144. Mrs. Maro Lester-Barker

145. Mr. Wilbur Lewis

146. Mr. Patricia C. Lightfoot

147. Mr. Harold G. Logan

148. Brigadier General Sharon K. Mailey

149. Ms. Carolyn M. Manning

150. Lois G. Marchbanks

151. Ms. Roslyn Marchbanks-Robinson

152. Mr. Lawyer A. Martin, Esquire

153. Dr. William E. Matory

154. Major (Retired) Donald W. Mauney, Jr.

155. Dr. James J. McCord

156. Lieutenant Colonel (Retired) Walter L. McCreary

157. Colonel (Retired) Norman A. McDaniel

158. Sergeant Dennis D. McDuffie

159. Ms. Yvonne G. McGee

160. Mr. Gustavus "G" A. McLeod

161. Mr. Artis R. McNeill

162. Captain Stephen E. Medley

163. Mr. George L. Millard, Sr.

164. Mrs. Mary Louis Mohr

165. Charles A. Moose

166. Elizabeth S. Morris, D.D.S.

167. Mr. J. Byron Morris

168. Mr. Rocardo L. Nesbit

169. Colonel Donald W. Newton

170. Mr. Thomas A. Norris III

171. Mr. Samuel O'Dennis

172. Mrs. Barbara E. O'Neal

173. Lieutenant (Retired) Ira J. O'Neal

174. Brigadier General (Retired) Norris W. Overton

175. Major Robert L. Owens, Jr.

176. Dr. Florence Parrish-St. John

177. Lieutenant Colonel (Retired) Warner K. Parsons

178. Chief Master Sergeant (Retired) John B. Patterson

179. William S. Peace

180. Dr. Stevens W. Pearce

181. Mr. James A. Pendegrass

182. Major (Retired) William F. Peterson

183. Claude Platte

184. Dr. Lorna M. Polk

185. Mr. James R. Poole

186. Colonel (Retired) Elliott Powers

187. Colonel (Retired) Clark T. Price

188. Mr. James W. Pryde, Sr.

189. Dr. William W. Quivers

190. Colonel Harold Ray

191. Colonel (Retired) William T. Reynolds

192. Mr. Samuel W. Rhodes

Tuskegee Airmen Wives Auxiliary (TAWA)

Established approximately 1980

In accordance with the transitions of society, the organization's name is being changed to that of the "Tuskegee Airmen Women's Auxiliary," in order to attract the interest of others who would further perpetuate its goals and standards.

Mission Statement

To assist the East Coast Chapter of the Tuskegee Airmen, Inc., in their efforts to inspire and motivate youth in pursuing aviation and aerospace careers, and to provide financial support through fundraising and other special projects.

Current Members

L. Peggy Bethel	Lourecka O'Neal
Corrine "Dimples" Boyd	Selma Rhodes
Claretta "Nancy" Carroll	Leontine Smith
Marietta Hughes	Mary T. Wade
Purnell "Penny" Lawrence	Linda Yancey
Ella McLease	

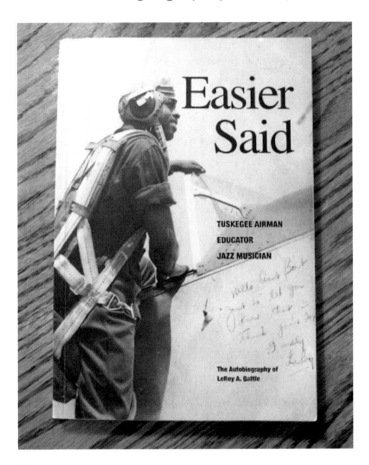